WALKS ALONG OFFA'S DYKE

Warne Gerrard Guides for Walkers

Walks for Motorists Series

CHESHIRE WALKS
CHILTERNS WALKS
Northern
Southern
CORNISH COASTAL WALKS
COTSWOLD WALKS
Northern
Southern
COUNTY OF AVON WALKS
COUNTY OF DURHAM WALKS
DARTMOOR WALKS
DERBYSHIRE WALKS
Northern
Southern
DORSET WALKS
ESSEX WALKS
EXMOOR WALKS
FAMILY WALKS IN MIDLAND COUNTIES
FOREST OF BOWLAND
FURTHER CHESHIRE WALKS
FURTHER DALES WALKS
GREEN LONDON WALKS (both circular and cross country)
HAMPSHIRE AND THE NEW FOREST WALKS
HEREFORD AND THE CENTRAL WELSH BORDERS WALKS
HERTFORDSHIRE WALKS
ISLE OF WIGHT WALKS
JERSEY WALKS
KENT WALKS
LAKE DISTRICT WALKS
Central
Northern
Western
LOTHIAN AND SOUTH EAST BORDERS WALKS
MIDLAND WALKS
NORTHUMBERLAND WALKS
NORTH YORK MOORS WALKS
North and East
West and South
PEAK DISTRICT WALKS
PENDLESIDE AND BRONTE COUNTRY WALKS
SEVERN VALLEY WALKS
SNOWDONIA WALKS Northern
SOUTH DEVON WALKS
SOUTH DOWNS WALKS
SURREY WALKS
WARWICKSHIRE WALKS
WYE VALLEY WALKS
YORKSHIRE DALES WALKS

Long Distance and Cross Country Walks

HEART OF ENGLAND
NORTH TO SOUTH ALONG THE PENNINE WAY
RAMBLES IN THE DALES
WALKING THE PENNINE WAY
WALKS ALONG OFFA'S DYKE

Warne Gerrard Guides for Walkers

WALKS ALONG OFFA'S DYKE

A FOOTPATH GUIDE

Compiled by
Ernest and Katherine Kay
on behalf of The Offa's Dyke Association

FREDERICK WARNE

First published by Spurbooks Ltd, 1977

This (revised) edition published 1983 by Frederick Warne (Publishers) Ltd,
40 Bedford Square, London WC1B 3HE

The photograph on the front cover shows a view of Llanfair Hill, Shropshire and was taken by Derek Forss.

At the time of publication all routes used in these walks were correct, but it should be borne in mind that diversion orders may be made from time to time. Maps are not necessarily to scale.

This new edition is dedicated to the memory of the late Jack Baker, Chairman of the Offa's Dyke Association at the time of his death in 1981. His work on footpaths, particularly in the Northern Marches and Cheshire, benefited and inspired innumerable other walkers. One of his last works was the revision of walks in the Oswestry area included in this book.

ISBN 0 7232 2824 8

Phototypeset, printed and bound by Galava Printing Co. Ltd., Nelson, Lancashire

Contents

			Page
		Introduction	7
		Notes—Public Transport, Maps, Length of Walks	8
		A Walker's Guide to Welsh Place Names	9
		Country Code	11
Area	1	Tintern Abbey and Woods; Brockweir	12
	2	Redbrook; Kymin and Monmouth; Staunton	17
	3	Longtown and Black Mountains	22
	4	South of Hay-on-Wye	29
	5	Presteigne	35
	6	Knighton, Stowe and Offa's Dyke Park	39
	7	West of Bishop's Castle; Kerry Hill Ridgeway	43
	8	Oswestry; Sweeney Mountain and Trefonen	48
	9	Llangollen, Valle Crucis, Eglwyseg and Dinas Bran	54
	10	Clwydian Hills	60
		Bibliography	64
		Some Useful Addresses	64

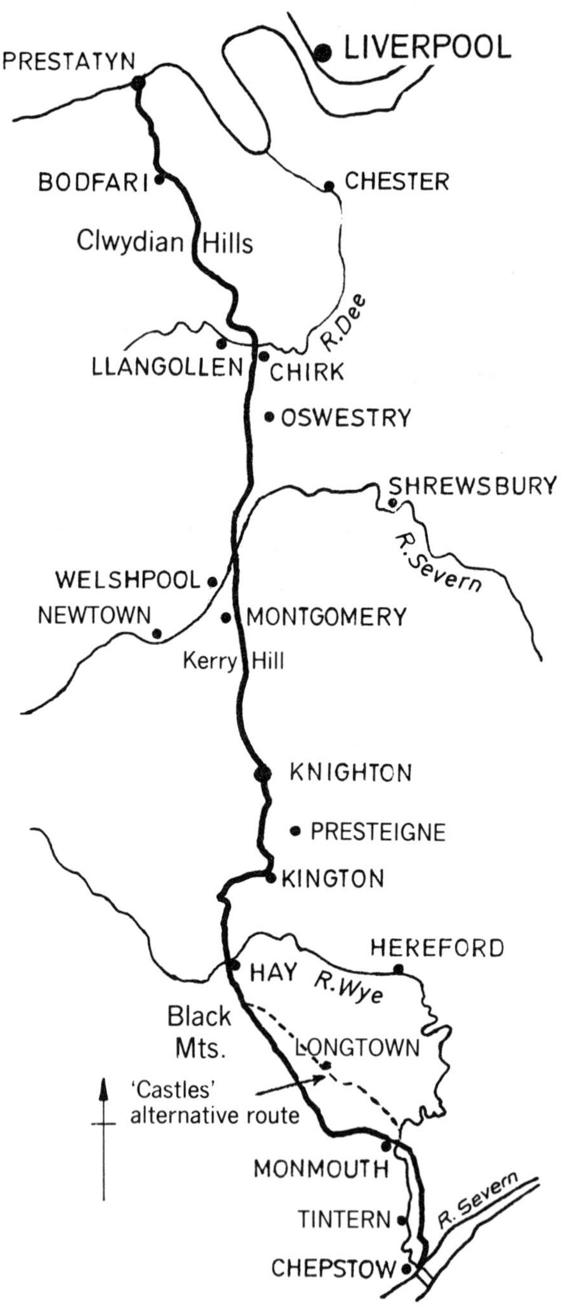

LIVERPOOL
PRESTATYN
BODFARI
CHESTER
Clwydian Hills
R.Dee
LLANGOLLEN
CHIRK
OSWESTRY
SHREWSBURY
R.Severn
WELSHPOOL
NEWTOWN
MONTGOMERY
Kerry Hill
KNIGHTON
PRESTEIGNE
KINGTON
HEREFORD
HAY
R.Wye
Black Mts.
LONGTOWN
'Castles' alternative route
MONMOUTH
TINTERN
R. Severn
CHEPSTOW

Introduction

Offa's Dyke is a great frontier earthwork built in the reign of Offa, King of Mercia, in the late eighth century to mark the boundary between his kingdom in Central England and the Welsh. It is still visible over some eighty miles of its length—in places upstanding to 20 feet from the bottom of the ditch to the top of the bank.

The name was used for a Long Distance Footpath officially opened in July 1971, which incorporated some sixty miles of the best of the remaining earthworks. The Path runs for 168 miles from Chepstow to Prestatyn, mostly through the varied and little frequented landscapes of the Welsh Marches and taking in the Black Mountains and the Clwydian Hills.

This book of circular walks, based on the Path, is compiled from material supplied by Members of the Offa's Dyke Association. This was set up in 1969 to co-ordinate pressure for the opening of the Path. This achieved, the Association has continued in order to bring together the many interests of walkers, historians and conservationists, and those who live and work locally, involved in looking after the Dyke and its Footpath. Its headquarters are at Knighton, Powys (the halfway point of the route) from which address details of membership, publications, accommodation etc. may be obtained.

Also based in Knighton in the same building as the Association is the Offa's Dyke Heritage Centre. Financed mainly by the Manpower Services Commission, this provides a public exhibition, a library and other study facilities and periodic short educational courses covering many aspects of Welsh Border life, landscape and history.

This book is divided among ten areas in each of which at least one longer and one shorter route are described. These may be variations on one basic route or entirely separate. They are but a sample of the walks that could be included; major centres such as Chepstow, Kington, Clun, Montgomery and Prestatyn have not been used at all. These routes are no substitute for walking the Long Distance Path itself but for many this is not possible and we hope we are at least giving the flavour of this unique Path and countryside.

Brief linking notes covering the Path between the sections used on the circular walks have been included in the text. Walkers on the round routes will have the advantage of seeing much more than the Path itself.

We are most grateful to Robin Cain, David Cole, Don Gregory, Arthur Roberts, and the late Jack Baker and Frank Noble who have joined with us in providing the material. We have not tried to impose a unity of style on our correspondents, merely to aim at a consistent level of information.

KATHERINE AND ERNEST KAY

Note to the Second Edition

We have received no reports of major difficulties or disappointments encountered by walkers using the First Edition, so the routes remain basically unchanged. A considerable number of variations, improvements and additions have been made, some ambiguities in the text have been clarified, and of course any known physical changes have been taken into account. The maps have been redrawn for greater clarity. The Offa's Dyke Association (Knighton, Powys, LD7 1EW) will continue to welcome any comments, suggestions or complaints!

K. & E.K.

Notes

Public Transport

Rail is relevant only to Areas 1 (Tintern from Chepstow), 6 (Knighton), and 8 (Oswestry via Gobowen). Please consult current British Rail timetables.

Buses are generally infrequent even where services do exist and are prone to withdrawal or alteration to timings. Most companies will supply timetables in return for s.a.e. though sometimes a small charge is involved. Timetables are seldom displayed in the towns and villages concerned. Names and addresses of companies mentioned in the text are:

National Welsh, 253 Cambridge Road West, Ely, Cardiff.
Yeomans Canyon Travel, Bus Station, Commercial Road, Hereford.
Primrose Motors, Dishley Street, Leominster, Herefords.
Teme Valley Motors, Leintwardine, Salop.
Owens Motors, Knighton, Powys.
Valley Motor Services, Bishops Castle, Salop.

Bryn Melyn Motors, Llangollen, Clwyd.
Vale of Llangollen Tours, Market Street, Llangollen, Clwyd.
Crosville, Crane Wharf, Chester.

Maps

These are diagrammatic and not to scale. Used with the text and in particular correlating the point indications—(1), (2), (3), etc.—they should enable walkers to find their route. Though expensive to purchase use of Ordnance Survey maps to supplement the sketch maps can be recommended and reference is made on each walk to the appropriate ones.

Length of Walks

These are given in 'miles' but 'hours' may be more appropriate as terrain can vary so much. Roughly regard two miles as one hour on unsurfaced routes, and three miles on surfaced, for an average walker.

Equipment

Offa's Dyke Path is 'real' though not 'difficult' walking and no special equipment is necessary. Walking boots, or at least shoes with properly ridged soles, are essential. A waterproof, spare warm clothing, emergency food and a compass are also 'musts'. A plastic map holder for your OS maps (and this guide book) will prolong their life.

A WALKER'S GUIDE TO WELSH PLACE NAMES

The Welsh language looks, to the English eye, like a collection of typographical errors and spelling howlers, all of which are quite unpronounceable. Less intrepid visitors give up what appears to be the unequal struggle of trying to pronounce place names correctly or discover their meanings. Thus they lose much of the charm of Wales. The names of villages, mountains and farms are the spice which gives any country its special flavour.

How to pronounce it

The anarchic, unpronounceable appearance of the Welsh language is caused by the fact that a small but crucial number of Welsh letters represent different sounds from those sounds which they present in English spelling. Take the letter W for example. In Welsh, W is almost always like the double OO in the English word 'moon'. The word *cwm* (a valley) is pronounced COOM. The west country word COOMBE is Welsh in origin and means exactly the same thing. Another problem is the letter F, which in Welsh is always pronounced as a V, as in the word *afon* (a river), which a Welshman pronounces as if it were spelt AVON. In fact, the River Avon in England gets its name directly from Welsh. If you want to write the sound of English F you must write FF in Welsh. A Welshman named Fred, for example, would spell his name FFred.

The letter Y is often pronounced like I in English words such as kit, it, bit etc. So the apparently unpronounceable word *twyn* (a small hill or burial mound) is pronounced TOO-IN. Otherwise, Y is pronounced rather like UH in English: *Twyn-y-gaer* is TOO-IN UH GUYER, fortress hill. In Welsh, the word *Y* means 'the'.

The double LL in Welsh place names fills many with alarm. But it really presents no problems. Properly speaking the double LL is pronounced by placing your tongue behind your front teeth and blowing slightly, making a hissing noise. But it is quite sufficient to pronounce it like the ordinary letter L in English (large numbers of Welsh people do).

A few other things to note: DD in Welsh is pronounced like TH in English. 'Though' in Welsh would be written '*ddo*'. The letter U is often pronounced as 'ee' in the English word bee. *Un* (one) is spoken as 'een'. Combinations of letter such as AE and AU are pronounced just like 'aye' in English; *Maes,* (a field) is pronounced the same as the English word 'mice'.

What does it mean?

Welsh place names are usually descriptions, some of them quite poetic. But the emphasis is on description. Many places begin with the word *aber*, meaning the mouth of a river. Aberyswyth, the mouth of Ystwyth River; Abertawe (the Welsh name for Swansea), the mouth of the Tawe River. Another class of place names begins with the world *Llan,* a church or parish. Llanfair, the church of (St.) Mary; Llanfihangel, the church of (St.) Michael.

Plurals in Welsh are usually formed by adding the letter AU to the end of a word. An example is *dol* (a meadow); *dolau* (meadows).

A small Welsh-English pocket dictionary would be a useful companion in any walker's rucksack. But for the impecunious here is a small glossary of common words and their meanings:

Glossary

Bach, fach, small
Bryn, Hill
Bwlch, Pass
Caer, Gaer, Fort

Cefn, Ridge
Clawdd, Dyke
Coed, Wood
Du, Black
Dwr, Water
Dyffryn, Valley
Llyn, Lake
Llys, Hall or Palace
Maen, Stone
Mawr, Fawr, Big
Melin, Mill
Nant, Stream
Pont, Bridge
Ty, House

Follow the Country Code

Enjoy the countryside and respect its life and work.
Guard against all risk of fire.
Fasten all gates.
Keep your dogs under close control.
Keep to public paths across farmland.
Use gates and stiles to cross fences, hedges and walls.
Leave livestock, crops and machinery alone.
Take your litter home.
Help to keep all water clean.
Protect wildlife, plants and trees.
Take special care on country roads.
Make no unnecessary noise.

Area 1 Tintern Abbey and Woods, Brockweir

(A) 10, (B) 7, (C) 5½, (D) 3½, (E) 2½ miles.

O.S. 1:50,000. 162; O.S. 1:25,000. SO 50.
Grid references are to these maps.

How to get there: By car: Tintern and Brockweir are on A466 Chepstow-Monmouth road. Tintern Abbey has a car park, some parking is possible at Brockweir, *none* at Bigsweir.

By public transport: Chepstow is the railhead, National Welsh (Wyedean) Chepstow-Monmouth bus serves all above points.

Refreshments: Tintern has full facilities; Brockweir a shop and public house; nothing at Bigsweir or elsewhere.

Offa's Dyke Path begins in the south at Sedbury Cliffs overlooking the Severn near Beachley and the new bridge. After 1 mile the east bank of the Wye is reached and this is followed leaving Chepstow (with its castle and other historic features; also transport and accommodation) just to the west. The route continues on the east of the Wye but the river is now some hundreds of feet below the well-marked Dyke and Path. The North-South routes of river and of Path and links between them are the subjects of the first walks, starting some seven miles from Sedbury.

These walks use a pair of circuits, a short one Tintern—Path—Brockweir—east bank of river and back, 3½ miles (route D), with a variant of similar length on the west bank (route E); and a longer one of Brockweir—Path—Bigsweir—river—Brockweir, 7 miles (route B) which can be joined into one 10 miles round (A). The longer circuit has a cut-off that can reduce it to 5½ miles (C); this Brockweir—Bigsweir stretch is unusual in having an 'official' alternative Path route. Our round uses both so you are following Offa's Path for the whole route!

Tintern Abbey
Starting at Tintern don't omit a visit to the ruins of the great Cistercian Abbey, (1) on map (533000). Owned now by the Department of the Environment it is open daily. The Abbey was founded in 1131 but most of what is visible is late 13th century. The remains of the church are most impressive, perhaps the East and West

AREA 1

Bigsweir Bridge
A466
Offa's Dyke Path
8
A, B
Bigsweir House
7
C
St. Briavels Hall
6
Sittingreen
PATH (main route)
The Fields
DYKE
A, B, C
Chapel
5
OFFA'S
N
RIVER WYE
OFFA'S DYKE PATH (alternative route)
A, B, C
Brockweir House
Stream
Brockweir
3
B, D, E
4
Tintern Old Station
Church
A466
E
A, D
OFFA'S DYKE
A, D, E
Gap
Car Park
Tintern Abbey
1
A, D, E
2
Offa's Dyke Path
Devil's Pulpit

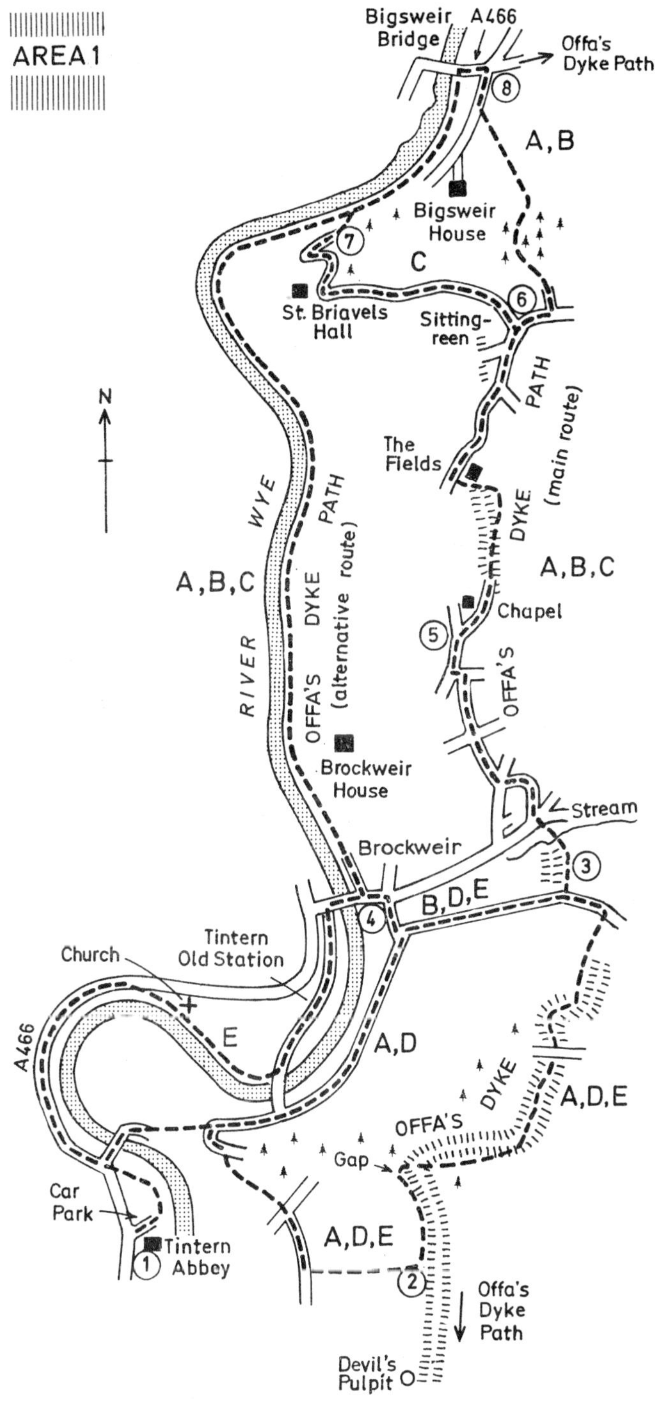

windows in particular.

Tintern itself is a small-scale tourist mecca but the route to Offa's Dyke soon leaves it. From car park at Tintern Abbey, leave by footpath near river passing to right of Anchor public house and follow through to main road at Police Station. Turn right, go along road a short distance and turn right past disused watermill along formation of disused Tintern Wireworks tramway, crossing river by metal bridge. In under 100 yards turn left up track with a small area of stone paving at its junction with the tramway.

Rise up to junction of tracks beside stone retaining wall on left: fork right up wide track, shortly fork right (sign to Devil's Pulpit painted on tree) and next left, following above and parallel to lane below, then curving away and climbing up to join forestry road. Turn right, then immediately left at junction of forestry roads where stone directs to the 'Devil's Pulpit'. In 150 yards fork left up an obvious track which leads uphill to join the clearly defined and way-marked Offa's Dyke Path at the top of the hill, (2) (542000).

(The *Devil's Pulpit* itself is reached by turning right along the Offa's Dyke Path for about ⅓ mile. It is a limestone crag just under the Dyke with fine views of the valley, including Tintern Abbey. By tradition, the Devil preached to the monks of Tintern from here. Return to point (2) to continue walk.)

Turn left to follow the Dyke north to where a modern gap has been cut through a prominent stretch of the earthwork. Pass through the gap and bear left to follow the Path with the Dyke on your left. After 200 yards cross a marshy gap and continue on the Dyke itself. Cross a farm lane, a short stretch further downhill, right and in a few yards arrow signs point your way steeply left through the woods and downhill away from the ridge. Follow the Dyke as a broad bank till where it is ploughed out and then bear right downhill to a gate in the corner of the field. Left through this to reach a vertical post, (3) (546013), indicating alternative Offa's Dyke routes—left and also bearing right through gate.

First the left route to Brockweir and back to Tintern: a broad track leads in half a mile to Townsend Farm and right into Brockweir village (4) (540011). Left at the farm, where Offa's Dyke Path turns right, through gate and follow unsurfaced lane forward for a mile with river views to right. Following a steep drop, where the lane is paved with stone for a small area, turn right to join the track of the disused Tintern Wireworks railway, in which the remains of wooden sleepers can be seen at intervals. Follow this over a metal bridge over the Wye to join the A466 by a disused watermill. Left on road to just beyond the Police station, left down a path signposted 'River Wye 0.2 km.' Shortly fork left past chapel and follow path into Tintern Abbey car park, (1), to complete route D.

Route E: Alternatively from (4) follow Offa's Dyke Path past Brockweir Inn. Cross bridge and immediately left down steps. Follow 'Wye Valley Walk' along disused Chepstow-Monmouth railway track (or take riverside option) to reach Tintern Old Station. This is now well laid out as a railway exhibition, publications and refreshments site. Continue on railway formation to site of old bridge, down steps to Wye and along bank. Through St. Michael's churchyard to A466 immediately west of the Wye Valley Hotel. Right along road for ½ mile, mostly with pavement, to reach the end of the 'Wireworks Footbridge'. (The two Brockweir-Tintern routes themselves make a short 2½ mile circuit.)

Forward and right through the gate at (3) (546013), the Path leads by small lanes and footpaths with intermittent Dyke to St. Briavel's Common and Bigsweir. This is an area of small farms and houses, well populated but with no villages. First downhill with Dyke on left to cross a small stream and up to the Brockweir-Hewelsfield road. Take lane almost opposite and follow it as it turns left over a stream; left at minor road and immediately sharp right—all this in a couple of hundred yards. The rather muddy lane you are now on emerges on to a road; left, soon swing right and take right fork, (5) (540023), past an old chapel. This road soon peters out and an enclosed path takes you steeply uphill. Left at top and through the farmyard of 'The Fields' (please keep to marked route and close gates) to road. 200 yards right along this and where road bends right take the lane straight ahead; this emerges on another road at Sittingreen, (6) (539038).

Offa's Dyke Path takes the right turn but alternatively the left turn may be taken and the gradually deteriorating road followed steeply downhill. At the bottom keep St. Briavels Hall on your left and pass between stone pillars to the river bank, (7) (531040). Turn left towards Brockweir and 1½ miles has been cut from the route (Route C).

The main route from Sittingreen does not keep to the road for long: take a narrow path left in a hundred yards. Right at a T junction of paths and in a few yards left to slope very steeply downhill through woods for ¼ mile. Continue in the same direction across a field and diagonally left down towards a stone bridge visible in the corner of the next field. Right along drive (left goes to 18th century Bigsweir House) to A466 at Bigsweir Bridge, (8) (540051).

Walk 25 yards towards the bridge and left across stile by the end of the bridge. Something under 3 miles of easy riverside walk will bring you to Brockweir at Quayside just east of the bridge. This stretch has excellent views across the river and up to the woods and there are no path problems. (After under 1 mile the short cut from Sittingreen to St. Briavels Hall described above is met). In Brockweir turn up the pleasant village street. First right, (4) (540011), leads to the way to Tintern described above which completes the full 10 miles circuit (route A).

(The 7 mile circuit (B) starts at Brockweir Street. First right, (4) (540011), to Townsend Farm and left to broad track to main Dyke Path at (3) (546013). Then left to Bigsweir and back to Brockweir as described).

So far the Path has followed good stretches of the historic Dyke on the escarpment high above the Eastern bank of the Wye. This continues North for nearly 4 miles beyond Bigsweir, almost to Highbury Farm. There, quite abruptly, the Dyke disappears and the Path drops down to the Wye at Redbrook. There is now a major gap in the continuous Dyke as far as Bridge Sollers, west of Hereford, and the Path does not pick it up again until north of Kington over 50 miles away. The next routes are set in the Wye Valley going North from Redbrook into Monmouth.

Area 2 Redbrook, Kymin, Monmouth, Redbrook 6 miles; with Newland extension 8 miles; Redbrook—Monmouth—Staunton circuit 10 miles (via river) or 11 miles (via Kymin)

O.S. 1:50,000. 162; O.S. 1:25,000. SO 51, 50 (Newland Extension only).
Grid references are to these maps.

How to get there: By car: Monmouth is on the A40(T) Ross-Abergavenny road, there is a large car park off Monnow Street near the old Monnow Bridge (505123); A466 connects to Hereford (north) and Chepstow (south). Redbrook is on this last road 3 miles south of Monmouth.

By public transport: National Welsh buses connect Monmouth to Newland, Redbrook and Chepstow, also Hereford, Ross etc.

Refreshments: Monmouth is a major town; Redbrook has pubs, shops and a cafe at the large garage on the west of the road, Newland and Staunton each have a pub and shop.

Offa's Dyke Path descends to Redbrook from the heights to the east of the Wye at Highbury Farm. The route then climbs the prominent hill of the Kymin (Naval Temple) on its way to Monmouth, an easy alternative follows the Wye going north from Redbrook. Combining these two makes an easy 6 mile round. (A) An extension takes in the Forest of Dean village of Newland with its 'Cathedral of the Forest'. (B) The route from Monmouth via The Biblins and Staunton to Redbrook is 7½ miles (C) and combines with either of the other routes between Redbrook and Monmouth.

From Wye Valley garage and cafe at Redbrook (1) (536102), cross A466 and take service road to left above main road and in front of houses. This passes between village houses and in 300 yards emerges on B4231 just above bridge over the road from an old colliery incline. Right up road and in ¼ mile take track forking left with cottage between road and track. In walking up the valley road you will have passed sundry ruined buildings from Redbrook's past as an industrial village in the Forest of Dean complex: in this case dependent on water power, the remains of furnace ponds are to be seen higher up the valley.

Follow track upwards as at the top of the slope it swings 90° to left, (2) (537108). Pass farm buildings (Duffields) on right and

AREA 2

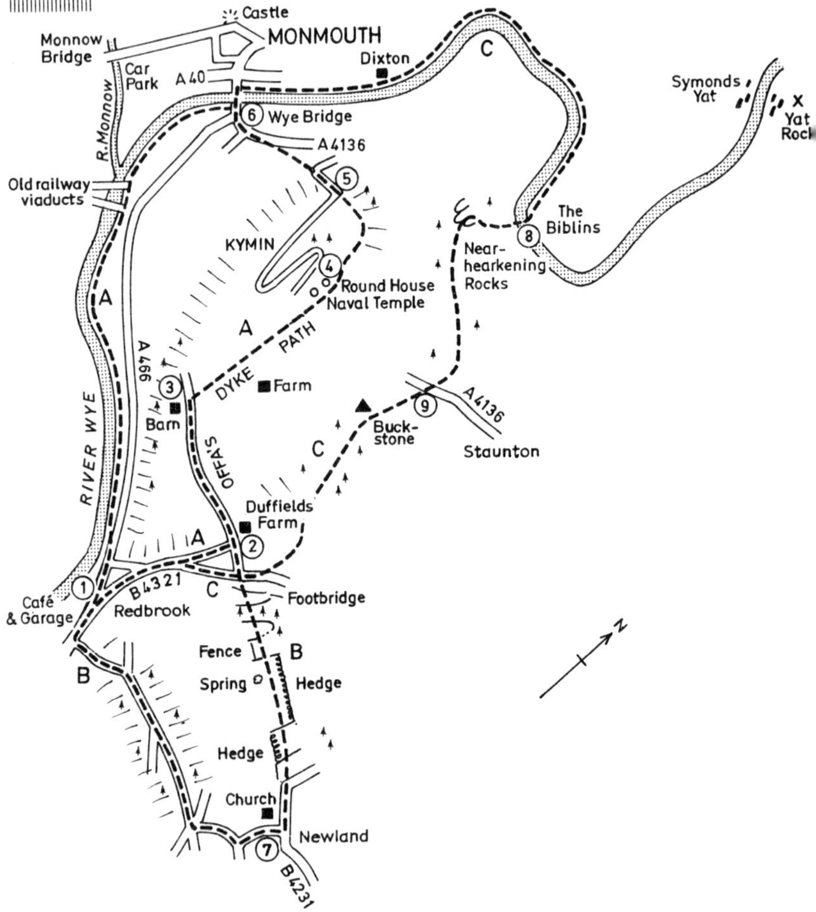

Castle
MONMOUTH
Monnow Bridge
Car Park
A 40
Dixton
C
Symonds Yat
X Yat Rock
R. Monnow
6 Wye Bridge
A4136
5
Old railway viaducts
The Biblins
8
KYMIN
4
Round House
Naval Temple
Near-hearkening Rocks
A
A
A 466
DYKE PATH
3
Farm
Barn
9
A4136
Buck-stone
Staunton
RIVER WYE
OFFA'S
C
Duffields Farm
A
2
1
Café & Garage
B4321
C
Redbrook
Footbridge
Fence
B
Spring
Hedge
B
N
Hedge
Church
Newland
7
B4231

continue to reach barn on left, (3) (530116). Opposite turn right over stile into field and aim uphill halfway between farm on right and trees on left. The path is not evident on the ground and keeping parallel to power line on right is the best guide. Cross stile in far corner of field and continue forward now keeping fence on left. Then through gate into wooded area to reach the National Trust owned area at the top of the *Kymin*. Cross car park and continue forward keeping the Naval Temple and Round House viewpoint on the left, (4) (528125)—but of course divert to visit them! The buildings were erected by members of a Monmouth dining club about 1800 in honour of the Royal Navy 'to perpetuate the names of those noble Admirals who distinguished themselves by their glorious victories for England in the last and present Wars.' It makes a pleasant place to pause for the view to the Black Mountains.

With the buildings on the left and still going northwards *avoid* the stile straight ahead but turn sharp left down stone steps. After about 200 yards cross stile on right and keep on downhill with fence now on left. Cross stile by large house and head diagonally right across large field. Cross into wood and swing left continuing downhill to come out on small road. (5) (523129), (this has zigzagged downhill from the top of the Kymin and can provide a bad weather alternative). Straight ahead on road and where this bends sharp right take footpath signposted Monmouth straight on. This emerges on A4136 five minutes walk from Wye Bridge, (6) (513127).

The riverside route back to Redbrook starts here; it is of course the beginning of the walk if done Monmouth—Redbrook—Monmouth. However most walkers will wish to see something of Monmouth and/or seek refreshment. The town has the *Shire Hall* in Agincourt Square with the *Castle* remains off Castle Hill just opposite (birthplace of Henry V, hence Agincourt!). *St Mary's Church* has a splendid tower but is mostly Victorian; the main street is wide and leads to the unique 13th century fortified gatehouse on the *Monnow Bridge*.

Returning to the riverside path the route will be seen clearly signposted Redbrook just to the east of Wye Bridge. Immediately keep to the right of a privet hedge by a sports pavilion and keep to the edge of playing fields. The path is clear thereafter by the riverside past former railway viaducts and a (not too obvious) sewage works. After over 1½ miles the A466 becomes a near-neighbour but the path continues in the fields by the river until joining the road quite near Redbrook village. Down the road to the Wye Valley garage and cafe. (1).

The Newland extension to the route (**B**) starts in Redbrook village.

From garage cross main road and turn right. Just past the church take slope and then turning left uphill between school and hall on narrow lane. This soon becomes unsurfaced and climbs steeply. Where it levels out take right turn at T junction with very broad track. In 200 yards take upper (left) fork by electric pump. Across the valley to your right Highbury Farm and the Dyke going south is evident. Climb slowly to junction of several paths. Take left enclosed unsurfaced track leading down (before starting on this, step a few paces to the right for a splendid view to Newland Church).

At the bottom the lane in 100 yards becomes surfaced. First left to pass between church on left and almshouses on right to B4231, (7) (553095). The church ('Cathedral of the Forest') is splendid and large for a tiny village; most of what is seen is 13th to 15th centuries with tombs and brasses. Turn left past the Ostrich, shop and bus stop. In 300 yards, past speed derestriction sign, turn left at 'Upper Redbrook' footpath signpost.

The paths on this next section are not visibly trodden out but by closely following this route walkers should not go astray. In the first field head diagonally across field to cross gate in angle on left. Forwards with hedge on left (do *not* get into woods on right). Just before top of rise cross gate on left and continue in same direction as before through several fields but with hedge now on right (beware of sticky patch at a spring). Eventually route crosses a stile and continues in the same direction with post and barbed wire fence on left (and splendid view up Kymin on right). Cross lower part of next field with wood below route on right; over stile and down into wood ahead. Cross fence (no obvious stile) into next field to stile and bridge to the B4231 at Upper Redbrook.

From Monmouth, another circuit walk continues north-eastwards along the Wye. From the south side of Wye Bridge (6) (513127) cross bridge and turn right on surfaced path waymarked 'Wye Valley Walk'. This soon becomes unsurfaced but continues on the river bank, in 2/3 mile reaching the interesting 13th century church at *Dixton*, Continue near the river through fields and then woods, eventually with rocky cliffs rising on the left.

In 3½ miles from Wye Bridge a campsite is reached at *The Biblins* (8) (548144). From here, the riverside path can be followed for another mile to reach *Symonds Yat*, the famous beauty spot. Here, the river can be crossed by a ferry, leading to a climb to the Yat Rock for spectacular views of the river valley; nearby is an earthwork described as Offa's Dyke on the Ordnance maps, though it may be an earlier Iron Age promontary fort.

For the circuit returning to Redbrook, from The Biblins (8), cross the footbridge to the south bank, turn left along the river for a short distance (this track, on the formation of an old railway, can also be followed to Symonds Yat), then turn right into the woods uphill, at first with a fence on the left. At a cross track turn right, swing slightly left at the next cross track and up to a Forestry track. Turn left on this but soon swing right and upwards to cross another wide track. Reach a T-junction of paths just below the summit ridge. Go right on a path soon swinging left to reach and cross a track on the summit ridge. Descend to *Nearhearkening Rocks* (wide views of the Kymin and west of Monmouth) and steeply down to the right of the rocks, then below them to the giant Suckstone and the Forestry track beneath.

Turn left and in ⅓ mile, before the bottom of the descent, take a path climbing left and soon passing a large stone on the left. Near the top of the ridge fork left to contour just under the summit. Eventually fork right to the A4136 road at the west end of *Staunton* village (left into the village for White Horse inn etc.) (9) (547127). Take the surfaced lane opposite and slightly to the right. Through a gate and follow a wall up on the right to a reservoir on your left and the enormous *Buckstone* to the right. Cross the ridge and continue downhill in the same direction to pass Buckstone Lodge on your right, cross a road, and make for the corner of a wood ahead on the right. Join a green track and follow it down to a drive, turn right past a house on the left and then swing left on a green track through the woods. Fork right down a steep path, cross a Forestry road and at the end of the wood, where the road and a large house are seen below, cross a stile on the left and go down to B4231 over a further stile and gate. Turn right on road to reach the A466 at Redbrook in under ½ mile.

Area 3 Longtown and Black Mountains

(A) 16, (B) 12½, (C1) 8½, (C2) 5½, (D) 4, (E) 7½ and (F) 3½ miles.

O.S. 1:50,000. 161; O.S. 1:25,000. SO 22, 23, 32, 33.
Grid references are to these maps.

How to get there: By car: Longtown is on a turning off the A465 Abergavenny-Hereford road; left at Pandy Inn 6 miles from Abergavenny, then 4 miles via Clodock. (Llanthony is also off the A465—turn left 1½ miles south of the above at Llanfihangel Crucorney).

By public transport: Very occasional Yeomans bus from Hereford bus station to Longtown.

Refreshments: Longtown has inns and village shops; Llanveynoe a miniscule shop 100 yards from the Church; Llanthony and Clodock have inns.

The Plain of Monmouth—between that town where Area 2 ended, and the Black Mountains—is not our favourite part of the Offa's Dyke Path. However, though fairly flat, it does have attractive villages such as Llantilio Crossenny (which has a splendid music festival each May) and the finest castle directly on the route—the mainly 13th century White Castle. With its moat and towers this is for many people a fantasy castle made real. Beyond this there are attractive link routes to be found between the Path and the isolated peak of Skirrid. An alternative route has been worked out northwards from Monmouth which misses out White Castle but takes in those at Pembridge, Skenfrith, Grosmont and Longtown on the way to the Black Mountains and generally keeps to higher ground. North of the A465 Abergavenny-Hereford road both routes climb to the ridges of the Black Mountains: the next walks are centred on Longtown and take in stretches of each.

Longtown is a remote, straggly village lying under the shadow of the Hatterrall Ridge of the Black Mountains to the west and with the end of the Cat's Back Ridge to the north. The *Castle* consists of a stone keep (of about 1300) on an earthen motte in a large rectangular enclosure pierced by the modern road; the ruins have been consolidated by the Department of the Environment.

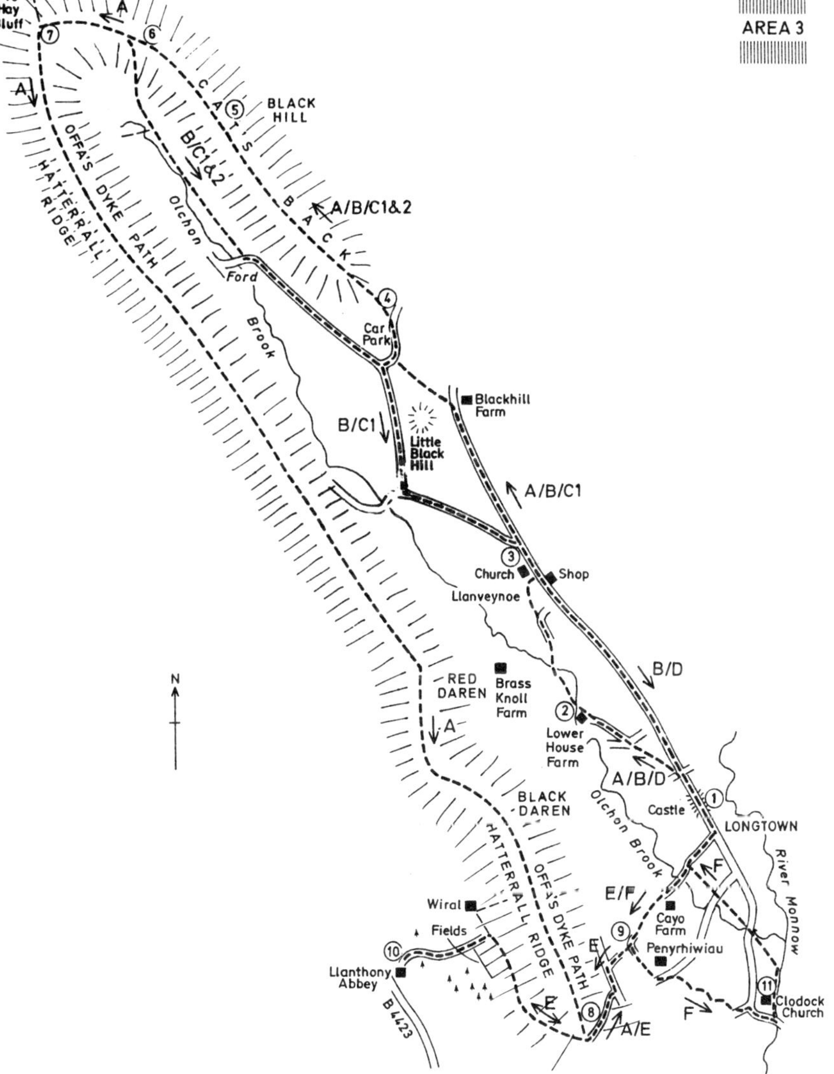

AREA 3
To Hay Bluff
BLACK HILL
CAT'S BACK
A/B/C1&2
B/C1&2
OFFA'S DYKE PATH
HATTERRALL RIDGE
Olchon
Ford
Brook
Car Park
Blackhill Farm
B/C1
Little Black Hill
A/B/C1
Church
Shop
Llanveynoe
B/D
RED DAREN
Brass Knoll Farm
Lower House Farm
A/B/D
Castle
LONGTOWN
Olchon Brook
River Monnow
BLACK DAREN
HATTERRALL RIDGE
OFFA'S DYKE PATH
E/F
F
Wiral
Cayo Farm
Fields
Penyrhiwiau
Llanthony Abbey
Clodock Church
A/E
E
B 4423
N

The complete round described below (Route A) is a splendid and very full day of 16 miles and only recommended for good walkers in fair weather with clear visibility since much of it is on the ridges of the Black Mountains. A variation cuts off 3½ miles (route B) and makes some of the remainder walking on minor roads. Route B itself splits into alternative circuits—of 8½ (C1) (with a 5½ mile variant (C2)) and 4 miles (D), the last being very simple. As a bonus the Longtown-Hatterrall-Llanthony walk is worth doing there and back (E-7½ miles) with a shorter round to Clodock (F-3½ miles). Longtown itself is on the 'Castles alternative' to the official Offa's Dyke route which runs north-south on the Hatterall and is used extensively on route A.

From Longtown Castle—routes (A), (B) and (D)—(1) (321293), walk north along the road for ⅓ mile. Beyond Perthi-Pertion, where there are cottages on both sides of the road, cross stone stile on left and head 45° right away from the road to pass through lower of two iron gates. Keep hedge on right, cross stile to surfaced lane, straight down this for 20 yards and then straight on through iron gate by corrugated iron shack. Bear left downhill on drive to Lower House Farm.

Circle round farm keeping buildings on left to reach stile crossing to path just above farmhouse, and down to cross footbridge over Olchon Brook, (2) (309303). Turn right with hollow way to left and stream to right. At waterfall bear slightly left to cross stone stile. Keep hedge on left through field and bear right away from Brass Knoll Farm in next field, then down to footbridge.

Cross corner of field heading upwards to cross stile (corrugated iron) and aim gradually uphill to stile to reach cart track. Where cart track bends right, cross old stile straight ahead in corner of field. Cross field towards Llanveynoe Church.

Leave field by gate in corner and out to road by track, (3) (304314). Turning right on this road the village shop and post office is reached in 100 yards and continuing takes one back to Longtown to complete route (D). Route (C1) *starts* on the road by Llanveynoe Church, where a car may be left, and picks up the route of walks (A) and (B), the start of which has been described above.

Coming out of the church, (3) (304314), turn left and after 150 yards take right fork at New House. This lane ends by Blackhill Farm; through gate straight ahead and after 20 yards through old gate on left. Bear right following fence on the right through old holly trees and take left of 2 iron gates. Continue uphill with old hedge on left to just below top of Little Black Hill. Through gate, turn right and reach metalled lane. Turn right along this (left returns to Llanveynoe and Longtown). In 150 yards car park and picnic site are reached (4) (288327). (The 8½ mile circuit (C1) can be reduced to 5½ (C2) while keeping the best of the view by starting the walk from here). Sign on left of car park says 'Black Hill, Offa's Dyke Path 4.8 km.' Cross stile as indicated by this and head upwards for the top of the ridge—the Cat's Back. Where ridge broadens take the right hand side.

Eventually the trig. point on top of Black Hill, (5) (275348), is reached. Bear slightly left keeping on top of the ridge with drop to your right for about ½ mile. The infant River Olchon may then be discerned in a distinct depression ahead and to the left of the track.

Before reaching this, if walking routes (B/C), (for route (A) see below), turn sharp left, (6) (266353), along a narrow track to reach the stream just above a ruined building. Do not take the path crossing the river at this point but continue downhill. Shortly, the Olchon Valley suddenly comes to view, and the path continues downwards, with the river to the right, in places quite steeply, for a further mile before joining the road. To the right will now be seen a picturesque grouping of ford and bridge: the route continues straight on down the road, a narrow, little-frequented lane with for some distance fine views to the right across the Olchon Valley. After a mile a lane to the left diverges to reach the picnic place and car park to complete route (C2): but if you continue along the little road for a further three miles you pass through Llanveynoe (completing route (C1) to reach Longtown (end of route (B)).

Route (A) continues forward from (6) (266353) and swings slightly left with steep drop on right. The trig point on Hay Bluff (Pen-y-Beacon) is soon visible in the distance ahead to the north-west; head for this. A mile short of it and a mile beyond the path leading to the Olchon Valley, meet the Offa's Dyke Path (7) (253360), descending on the left from the end of the Hatterrall Ridge, at a crossing of paths. There are no signposts. Turn left (note prominent rock outcrop on right) to climb 100 feet steeply south-east to the brow of the ridge; it is worth carrying a compass.

Once on the ridge, the route is to the 2306ft summit over a very boggy plateau area where the pressure of walkers has worn the surface away over a wide area. At the end of the main summit ridge a wooden post is seen and soon after a vertical boundary stone. The route descends to a col with a steep east edge visible ahead (Red Daren). Over a small rise another wooden post is reached at a cross path. Rise again, the path now swinging slightly right keeping to the top of the wide ridge and eventually rising to a trig point at 2010 feet.

Soon descend to a col with a vertical stone painted with acorn signs, then rise again to top of ridge behind Red Daren. The path surface is now much improved, grassier with less bog. Ascend to large cairn behind Black Daren and the path now begins to swing right and to descend. The next landmark is a cross path with the west route most evident—the Loxidge route to Llanthony. There are views to Longtown on your left, Skirrid ahead, and Sugar Loaf half-right. Descend slightly, then up to the next trig point (1810 feet). Drop down good turf track to a col with a crossing path (8) (308270), *seven* miles from the start of your walk on the ridge. The path on the right leads down to Llanthony, visible in the valley of the Honddu. Take the path leading steeply diagonally downhill on the left, which can be followed to Longtown as in the return leg of walk (E) below.

Route (E): A 7½ mile walk with Llanthony Abbey as its destination and involving a stiff climb across the Hatterrall in both directions, starts south down the road from Longtown Castle. Then, just beyond the Northants County Education Authority's Field Centre, turn right down a road marked with a T sign. Follow this across the river Olchon, through to Cayo Farm and pass to the right of the farm buildings. The route then runs uphill through fields with the hedge on the right. In the second field the route to Clodock (route F) bears to the left, (9) (313283), on a marked track.

For Llanthony, carry on up to a prominent line of trees crossing the path. Go through the gap in the line of trees at the right hand edge of the field, diagonally across the next field, and through iron hurdles into a short lane, with trees on each side, on the right. At the end of the lane go through a wooden gate, up a bank, and you come to a well defined cross track. Turn left, and after about 200 yards, just before the scanty ruins of a building, take the track on the right slanting uphill between trees. Follow this diagonally up the mountain to reach Offa's Dyke Path on the ridge (8) (308270). You have now climbed 1,150 feet from the River Olchon.

Cross Offa's Dyke Path and descend on a clear track, soon with a wall on the left. Slightly slope to the right and continue on a shelf above the woods when the wall peters out. Pass a wooden memorial cross on the right and over a small stream (with falls to the right). The path is now level with a fence on the left, crossing further small streams. Presently you come to three small fields on the left of the path: turn left after these down a track which leads through a narrow wood to the considerable ruins of Llanthony Abbey (10) (288277). The ruins of the largely Norman Transitional priory of Augustinian Canons are extensive. The Abbey Inn in the ruins and the Half Moon Inn 200 yards right up the main road provide less spiritual refreshment.

Returning to Longtown by the same route is very pleasant, giving quite a different set of views. On top of the Hatterrall Ridge (point (8)) route (A), see above, joins you for the descent to Longtown. An alternative way to this point from Llanthony is to ascend to the first of three fields referred to, then turn left to Wiral (instead of right). Just before the farm take track sharp right uphill. Where this peters out continue in the same direction to reach the summit ridge by a trig point. Right and in ½ mile point (8) is reached.

Route (F) is a short round walk Longtown-Clodock. It is not all well marked but is quite practicable provided care is taken. Start the same way as route (E) as far as point (9), two fields beyond Cayo Farm.

Follow the track diagonally across the field, left handed coming from Longtown, go into the next field, passing above small disused quarry and over stile, then just to right of a pond with larch trees around it, left where track from right is joined, to pass through iron gate into farmyard (Penyrhiwiau), then immediately right through another gate, past bungalow on left, then left down a sunken road.

At the first gate on the right where road drops, enter the field ahead, and leave it through a gap in the opposite hedge, diagonally to the right. In the next field there is a stone slab forming a rudimentary stile in the bottom right hand corner. Cross this, turn left, and keep hedge on left for the next two fields. When you come to three iron gates, go through the central one and cross the next field diagonally, aiming to the right of Clodock Church which is plainly visible. Go through iron gate, in 20 yards over stile on left, across a small dingle, diagonally across corner of field over stile and onto the road. Many of the stiles on this route are formed by a large flat slab of stone bedded on its edge.

Turn left along the road to the church, (11) (327275), which is worth a visit for its unusually complete early 18th century furnishings and fittings in a Norman setting.

Continue along the Walterstone Road and turn left just before the bridge over the River Monnow. The path runs between churchyard and river, along the river bank, then through orchards to reach the road again at the bridge over the River Olchon. Turn right across the bridge, then immediately left to follow the path near the river, passing across a lane, to the right of the sewage works, and turn right where it joins the outward route at the next lane.

Turn left at the main road in about 300 yards to bring you back to

Longtown Castle.

(Longtown — Llanthony — Clodock — Longtown joining routes (E) and (F) is a 9 mile alternative).

Area 4 — South of Hay-on-Wye

9 miles or 4½ miles

O.S. 1:50,000. 161 (**not** 148); O.S. 1:25,000. SO 23 & 24.
Grid references are to these maps.

How to get there: By car: Hay can be reached from Hereford via the A438; from Cardiff via Merthyr and Brecon; from the North via Leominster. There are adequate car parks, the largest behind the castle off Oxford Road (229423).

By public transport: Hereford is the railhead. Buses—Yeomans and National Welsh—are not frequent. There is also a service from Brecon.

Refreshments: Hay is well served with accommodation and a full range of refreshment places. Nothing else on the routes.

The last chapter had us walking in the Black Mountains above Longtown. According to which of two alternatives is used, the Path reaches the Northern summit ridge either just East of or at top of Pen-y-Beacon (Hay Bluff). From here there is a magnificent view northward over the upper Wye Valley (the same Wye as at Chepstow!) and into the South Radnor uplands. Underneath you is the Hay-Capel y Ffin mountain road and then the farmed slopes leading down to Hay-on-Wye. The next walks are in this area between the mountains and Hay and are best approached from the latter.

The Town:

There is no evidence of a settlement at Hay until the closing years of the 11th century. The name 'Hay' derives ultimately from the Norman-French word 'la haie', a hedge. When Bernard de Newmarch, a Norman Baron, began his conquest of the old Welsh kingdom of Brycheiniog (from which the modern name Brecon originates), he appears to have granted the land round Hay to one of his followers, another Norman named William Revell. Revell established a simple castle and a church on the site of modern Hay in the early years of the 12th century.

Within a few decades the original castle was replaced with a larger stone-built one a few hundred yards to the east—a structure which still survives, although in a fragmentary state. At the foot of this

AREA 4

Clock Tower
1
St. Mary's Ch.
Castle
HAY-ON-WYE
Car Park
Almshouses
B4350
2
Cemetery
Cusop
OFFA'S
Dingle
WALK)
HAY COMMON
Pen Common
6
DYKE
(SHORT
Upper Dany Forest
Pen-yr-hen-allt
3
Penyrwrladd Cairn
Cadwgan Farm
FOREST
PATH
To Hay
Dany Capel
N
5
Twyn y Beddau
To Penlan
4
Offa's Dyke Path to Hatterrall Ridge
To Capel y Ffin

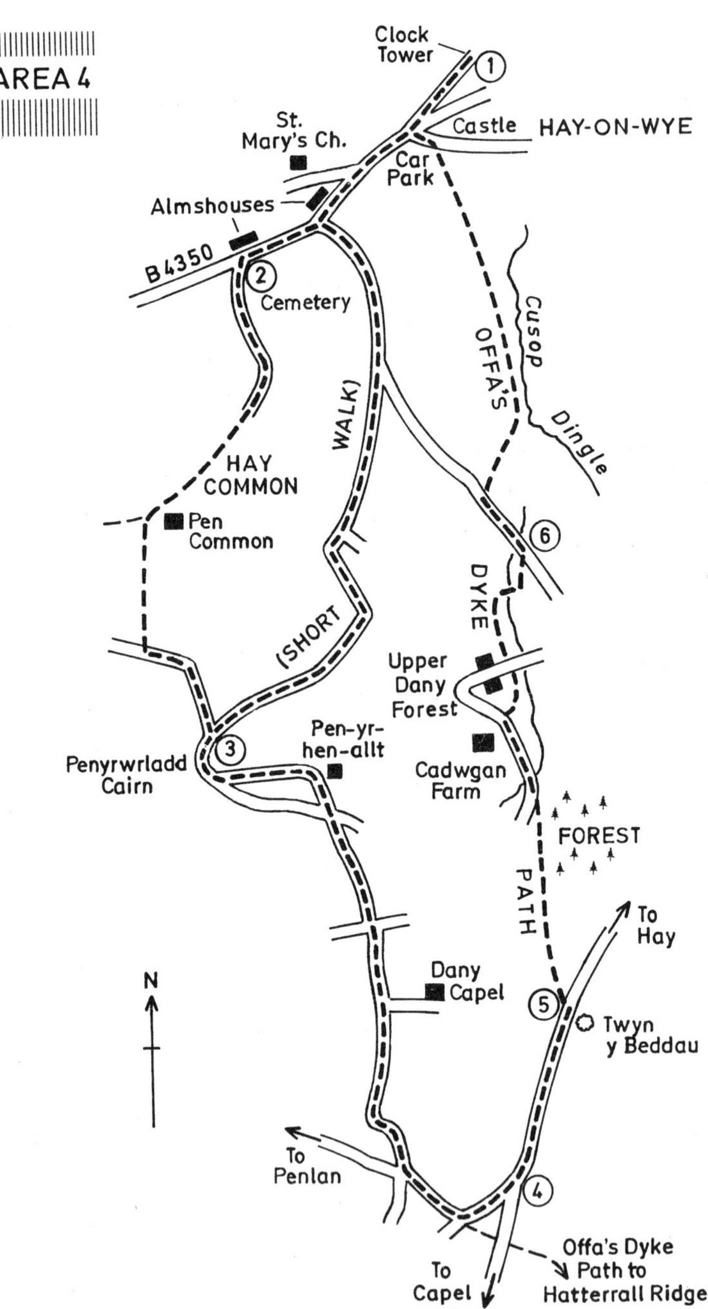

second castle a walled town was built, enclosing about 60 acres and reaching right down to the banks of the Wye—'one of the most compact military strongholds on the Welsh Border.'

There is no doubt that Hay's main reason for existence in the earliest days *was* military: to secure and hold recently conquered territory and to control movement along the Wye Valley. As such, the town and castle were frequently fought over, captured, burnt: by King John in 1216; by Llewelyn the Great in 1231; possibly by Owain Glyndwr in the last bid for Welsh independence in 1402.

Today there is little left of the original castle and the town walls and gates have disappeared completely. With the ending of the Welsh wars, Hay became a quiet market town. Today it is best known as the centre for the 'world's largest' second-hand bookshop. This has been followed by many other bookshops, and the avid reader should allow at least half a day to explore these!

The Walks:

There are two walks described here, both of them circular walks starting and finishing in Hay, the shorter covers about 4½ miles; the longer covers nearly 9. Both show to good advantage what Hay and the foothills of the Black Mountains have to offer in the way of unspoilt scenery and intriguing history. Since both walks start off the same, they will be described together.

Start from Hay Clock Tower (1) on map (229425) in the centre of Hay and set off up the main street (Belmont Road, the B4350 to Glasbury, Brecon and West). At the top of the hill you will pass on your right a small cafe which occupies the site (or near enough) of the old West Gate of the walled town of Hay. And a little beyond, and also on your right, is a castle mound, probably the site of William de Revell's first castle. Just beyond is St Mary's Church. Founded in 1120, it is as old as the town itself. Carry on along the B4350 past two groups of early 19th century almshouses built in the 1830's 'for the reception of ... poor, indigent women'. On the left hand side of the main road opposite the second terrace of almshouses is the entrance to the town cemetery, a lychgate set back from the road, (2) (226419). Just to the right is a track curving away out of sight skirting the edge of the cemetery. This used to be the Offa's Dyke footpath; the route was changed in 1982 but it is still a public footpath. You will join the official path later in the walk. You turn left off the main road here and join the track. After a slow start the track begins to climb. The cemetery is on your left behind a high hedge. The banks on either side of the track get higher and higher as you carry on; the gorge of the small stream trickling alongside the track begins to take on impressive dimensions; the trees on either side of you grow together over your head.

After about half a mile the track comes to a gate. Go through and you are in an open place; this is the edge of Hay Common. Carry on following the track as it angles across to the left slightly and then turns sharply uphill. Keep the big hedge just on your right hand. In the distance the small building you see is Pen Common Cottage. The Common itself is on your left. The humps and bumps in the ground are all that remains of a once thriving community, for this is a classic example of a deserted Medieval village—settlements like it are known throughout Britain. It used to be thought that the Black Death in the 14th century was responsible for desertions of villages. And although the role of the plague must not be discounted, we know now that rapacious landlords, war and changing agricultural practice played a part in the years between 1100 and 1500.

Carry on up to Pen Common Cottage, turn right just before it, and after 50 yards turn left and carry on uphill, keeping the hedge on your left. Cross stile beside a gate and the path turns once again into a track. As you top the rise to this gate, you find the Black Mountains looming large before you. They contrast markedly to the gentle Wye Valley and the Hills of Elfael at your back.

The Black Mountains derive their name from their curious colour and not, as some have suggested, through any reference to the Black Arts, those most Welsh of Welsh things: magic and witchcraft. Still, many spine-tingling local legends about the Black Mountains have filtered down to modern times. Perhaps the most quietly sinister are the tales concerning the Old Lady of the Black Mountains, who lured travellers to their deaths in mists and at night. Those who had no alternative but to cross the mountains were advised to place a bowl of water at the foot of the maypole at nearby Craswall to ward off the attentions of the Old Lady.

Mindful that you have taken no such precautions, press on carefully down the lane. In a few hundred yards you join another roughly metalled track. Turn left, then swing right through another gate. Soon you should come to the remains of Penyrwrladd chambered cairn. Originally a cairn 60 feet long and half as wide, it concealed two burial chambers, both of them made of slabs of stone. The monument dates from the Neolithic (the New Stone Age) and was in use some 4,000 years ago. A few yards beyond the cairn you join a metalled lane, (3) (226397).

If you are taking the shorter walk, turn left down the lane and follow it down into Hay. The walking is easy and you are unlikely to meet any traffic beyond the occasional tractor.

If you are taking the longer walk, turn right at the lane and follow it uphill for about a mile and a half, passing Dan y Capel farm and a right-hand turning for Penlan and on until it emerges onto open moorland and then joins the road from Hay to Capel y Ffin. (4) (241379) Here you turn left and follow the lane downhill. This is as near as you will get to the Black Mountains on this walk though the route up to Hay Bluff, altitude 2,219 feet, the promontory nearest you, is obvious. The next one, looking west, is Darren Lwyd. (The Tumpa) which is 2,263 feet high. Between the two is Gospel Pass, through which the lane you are standing on passes on its way to Llanthony Priory and the enchanted Vale of Ewyas.

But you are going the other way, down the lane. Soon an acorn sign on a stone beside the road tells you that you have now joined the Offa's Dyke Path, which you will follow back to Hay. The mound you pass is Twyn y Beddau, Welsh for 'The Hillock of the Graves'. It is almost certainly a Bronze Age tumulus dating from the second millenium BC. Local tradition, however, claims the mound and the area round it as the site of a particularly bloody battle fought in 1093 between Rhys ap Teudwr, the last independent ruler of South Wales, and an English army. Rhys was killed along with thousands of his followers and the nearby Dulas Brook is said to have run red with blood for three days.

Just beyond Twyn y Beddau, (5) (242387), fork left off the lane, and, keeping the large forest of conifers just on your right, carry on downhill through a gateway and into a narrow lane. You ford a stream before passing Cadwgan Farm (a lovely old farmhouse) where the lane becomes surfaced as it picks its way down a very steep slope. Just beyond the farm, cross a stile on the right of the lane and cross diagonally to the lower side of the field to the right of an old incomplete hedge boundary. Take a track sloping steeply down to the right, then swing left and continue down to reach a stile just right of Upper Dan y Fforest farm. Turn left on lane, then immediately right over a stone stile. Continue down over three more stiles, hugging the left bank of a small stream. Eventually you will come to a footbridge, and after crossing it, turn left on the right bank of the stream to reach another surfaced road (6) (237408). Turn left and follow the road for about 400 yards, past a fine holly hedge, coming finally to a stile on the right hand side of the lane. Go over into the meadow and angle across it to the left to a stile in the corner. From here, the path moves down Cusop Dingle on the left bank of Dulas Brook. The Dingle is thickly wooded but it is possible to make out the houses of Cusop village through the trees.

You are in Wales here, looking across into England. The path is clear and leads through kissing gates and past doleful ponies, right to Hay. Up a narrow alley between buildings—you emerge, blinking, by the car park at the foot of Hay Castle.

On its way North from Hay the Path leaves the Wye to climb attractive valleys and hills to the hamlet of Newchurch and then the village of Gladestry. Over Hergest Ridge and then into the market town of Kington beyond which we pick up the Dyke again for one of the very best stretches of the route.

Area 5 — Presteigne

10 miles, with two possible short cuts reducing it to 6½ miles.

O.S. 1:50,000. 148: O.S. 1:25,000. SO 26, 36.
Grid references are to these maps.

How to get there: By car: B4360, 4362 from Leominster, B4355 from Knighton.

By public transport: Primrose bus from Leominster and Hereford; Owens from Knighton (all infrequent).

Refreshments: Presteigne has full facilities, shop at Norton.

The walks so far have looked at two areas in the lower Wye Valley and two in the Black Mountains. We now move north to the 14 splendid miles of Path in Radnorshire, mostly on or by the fine Dyke, from Kington to Knighton. Many attractive circular walks can be found in this stretch: here is described one long one (with short cuts A and B) linking Presteigne with the route.

Presteigne, on the Lugg, is the old Radnorshire shire town. Somehow it is more 'English' than most border towns with its handsome Georgian houses and Norman/Decorated church.

Leave Presteigne town centre. (1) (314644) via Broad Street, pass church, cross river; road is now called Ford Street. Pass Stapleton House in under 200 yards on right; just after this cross the stile on the left opposite a white house. Diagonally cross two fields: second field on slightly raised path. Turn left across stream on bars of stile. Diagonally cross field near two large trees to reach stile (under electricity cables). Turn left into lane for under ¾ mile.

Cross stream by bridge and immediately on right cross stile, keeping stream on right, go through gap in hedge. Go through gate to left of Sewage Works and another gate ahead (at far end of Works). Keep in same direction (hedge on left), passing farm on right. At end of field cross stile (houses on left) and continue forward on small road, (stream below on right). Road turns left and joins B4355.

Turn right (north) along main road past Norton Church, (2) (304673) on right (shop is on the left). Continue for ¼ mile on main

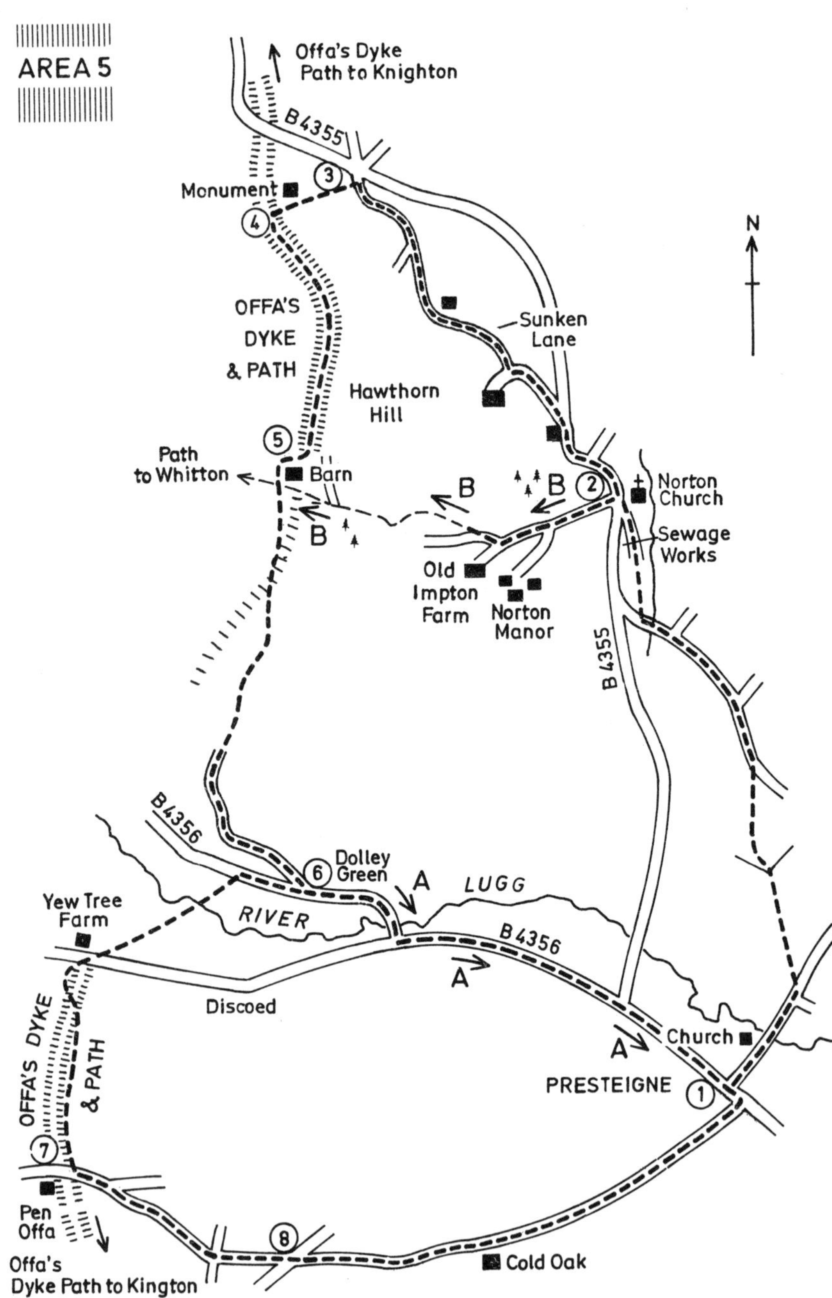
AREA 5
Offa's Dyke
Path to Knighton
B4355
3
Monument
4
OFFA'S
DYKE
& PATH
Hawthorn
Hill
Sunken
Lane
N
5
Path
to Whitton
Barn
B
B
2
Norton
Church
B
Sewage
Works
Old
Impton
Farm
Norton
Manor
B 4355
B4356
6
Dolley
Green
A
LUGG
RIVER
Yew Tree
Farm
B 4356
A
Discoed
A
Church
PRESTEIGNE
1
OFFA'S DYKE
& PATH
7
Pen
Offa
Offa's
Dyke Path to Kington
8
Cold Oak

road, which turns right and climbs, to 50 yards past cottage on left and turn through gate into metalled track on left and contour. Keep on metalled track until it bears sharp left to nearby farm buildings, then take sunken lane straight ahead. (The sunken lane is often obstructed, wet and uneven; an easier alternative is to follow green track on its left side for three fields with gates between, before rejoining track by a gate into it at the point where it becomes less sunken, more level and easier to use.). Follow track towards farm ahead, eventually passing in front of farm on right. Turn right by side of farmhouse on to metalled road which climbs and eventually joins B4355, (3) (287688). (Hill House entrance is opposite). Turn left through gate **just** before joining road onto track between two hillocks. A monument in the form of an obelisk can be seen ahead. Below Monument, to Sir Richard Green Price (1803-87) who brought railways to Radnorshire, bear left to stile on Offa's Dyke Path, (4) (285687). Do not cross this stile, but turn left (south) on line of Dyke.

Cross next stile to west side of Dyke. Path continues on Dyke, which is a well marked feature, up Hawthorn Hill and comes down gradually on west (right) side of hill past a corrugated iron barn, (5) (283674) on well signposted track. Continue with wire fence on right until just above plantation, where path strikes across field past sign-post and downhill, cross a stile, go through two iron gates, the second leading into a green lane between overgrown hedges. Continue down enclosed track to B4356 at Dolley Green, (6) (284655).

Turn right on road and in about 100 yards take track on left into field. Continue on left side of field to footbridge, and on left side of next two fields to cross road at Yew Tree Farm. The Dyke here becomes a massive feature with a deep ditch on the west. The path continues on the top of the Dyke uphill to lane at Pen Offa Bungalow, (7) (269639). (Just beyond the road, an original gap through the Dyke can be seen).

Leaving Offa's Dyke Path at Bungalow turn left along road to green lane about 100 yards on right through gate. After a time left hand hedge peters out but lane continues along right hand hedge to gate at green lane cross roads. Continue straight ahead between wire fence and hedge to junction with metalled road, (8) (282633). Turning left along road continue on it to Presteigne (about 2 miles) avoiding all side roads etc. and passing County Primary School on left on outskirts of town. By Green near housing estate take left fork to Clock Tower and Town Centre, (1) (314644).

Two **short cuts** save 2 and 1½ miles respectively on this route.

First (A) by turning left down the B4356 at Dolley Green, (6), Presteigne may be pleasantly reached in just over 2 miles.

For the second (B) leave Norton by minor road on left opposite church at point (2) and follow lane forward through gates, passing drive to Norton Manor on left, for nearly a mile until Old Impton Farm, a half-timbered building, is reached. Forward through gate leaving farm on left and in 30 yards take faint grass track on right, straight ahead across a junction of metalled tracks and cross field, leaving three large trees to your right, to reach iron gate. Go through gate and follow well-marked track, forking left at end of small conifer plantation, through gates, climbing steeply with sharp drop to left. Cross field at top of hill, ignoring well marked track bearing to right in field, to join Offa's Dyke footpath on left of corrugated iron barn near sign post, (5) (283674).

The northmost stretch of the above route (by the Green-Price monument) is little over two miles from Knighton, which may be reached by the Path following good Dyke all the way. About halfway, near Jenkin Allis Farm, the best preserved of the original gateways through the Dyke can be seen.

Area 6 Knighton, Stowe and Offa's Dyke Park

8 miles and 3 miles.

O.S. 1:50,000. 148 or 137; O.S. 1:25,000. SO 27 and 37.
Grid references are to these maps.

How to get there: By car: A488 from Shrewsbury and north; A4113 from Hereford and Ludlow. Large car park behind Norton Arms in town centre (286723).

By public transport: 5 trains daily (except Sundays) on Central Wales line – Shrewsbury to Swansea. Bus service, several a day (Teme Valley) from Ludlow and, more irregularly, (Owens Motors), Newtown and Presteigne.

Refreshments: Knighton has ample facilities, accommodation etc.

Knighton (Tref-y-Clawdd, i.e. the 'town on the Dyke' in Welsh) is the halfway point on both Path and Dyke. A compact and unassuming little market town, it has a special place in our affections as the setting for the official opening of the Long Distance Path in 1971 by Lord Hunt and as the centre for most Offa's Dyke activities, including the Association. The castle flourished in the 12th and 13th centuries (now a large mound at the top of the town) and the church tower is medieval. Offa's Dyke Park, the work of the local Tref-y-Clawdd Society, is off West Street and includes a fine stretch of Dyke. The old Primary School by the Park has been converted for use as a Youth Hostel and also houses the Offa's Dyke Association office and Information Centre and the Offa's Dyke Heritage Centre.

The town, set in the deep valley of the Teme, is a good walking centre. Here is one very pleasant route, (B) with a short alternative, (A), set to the north of the town; the ODA have published several others.

From Norton Arms, (1) (286723) take Station Road opposite past Knighton Station. Turn right on Clun road (A488). After 50 yards take green track on left which continues just above the road through lower part of Kinsley Wood. Where path meets horseshoe bend of metalled track, (2) take lower arm for longer walk 'B' (the short walk 'A' takes the upper arm).

At the next bend, (298728), go straight ahead over stile and across field towards big hedge in field beyond, crossing a footbridge.

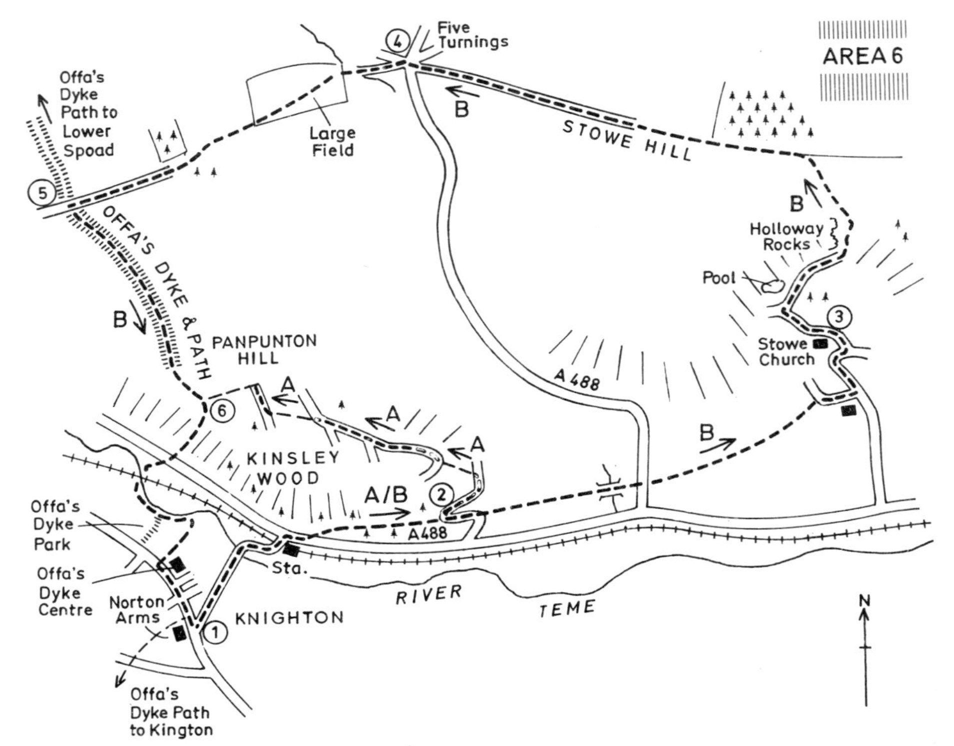
AREA 6
Five Turnings
Offa's Dyke Path to Lower Spoad
Large Field
STOWE HILL
Holloway Rocks
Pool
Stowe Church
OFFA'S DYKE & PATH
PANPUNTON HILL
A 488
KINSLEY WOOD
A/B
Offa's Dyke Park
Offa's Dyke Centre
Norton Arms
Sta.
KNIGHTON
RIVER TEME
Offa's Dyke Path to Kington
N

Take stile to road (A488) and iron gate opposite, proceeding with hedge on left. Go through series of gates; after first field, hedge is on right. (Views back to Kinsley Wood).

At top of ridge go through wooden gate and descend by hollow way directly opposite to broad unsurfaced farm track— right on this till it meets surfaced road—turn left up to *Stowe Church*, (3) (311737) (St. Michael) (Pevsner in 'Buildings of England' refers particularly to the beautiful setting, and says the masonry is medieval, the dressings renewed. He mentions also the good wooden roof, and an 'Arts and Crafts' reredos of 1901).

Continue on track circling to north-west behind church. At head of cwm near old quarry, go through wooden gate on right and take principal track forking right. Continue up valley (views back to Knighton and Radnor Forest). Bend right above pool on left, and continue upwards on track. Go through iron gate, circle left and then right, keeping in valley bottom as it climbs through Holloway 'Rocks'.

Emerge onto the green turf of Stowe Hill with new woodland a short distance to right. Turn slightly left over crest of hill due north (no visible track). Just over summit, reach wire fence by woodland, turn left along it and continue with fence on right through gates. (At end of woodland, fine views to right to Caer Caradoc hillfort in near distance and Stretton Hills beyond). After about 1 mile on ridge, track becomes enclosed lane—continue on this to main road (A488) at Five Turnings, (4) (286754).

Cross main road to grass track through iron gate opposite (**not** gate marked New House Farm). A short distance up track cross gate and muddy area into large field. Cross field diagonally (no clear path) to junction of two belts of woodland at top corner. Continue in south-easterly direction on green track with hedge on left, trees on right. Cross iron gate. 200 yards beyond, Offa's Dyke and the Long Distance footpath crosses track at belt of trees, (5) (276749). Turn left over stile with 'acorn sign'. (Views to Knucklas Viaduct and Castle to west are excellent).

It is two miles from here into Knighton and no difficulties should be found in following the route. The Dyke, though never very pronounced, is your constant companion and the Path is well used and quite clear—but you will have a lot of stiles to climb. You will soon reach Panpunton Hill which is the highest point visible from Knighton and where friends of the late Frank Noble, founder of the Offa's Dyke Association, have recently placed a seat in his memory.

The route now starts to descend and just before reaching the end of Kinsley Wood, (6) (285735), it turns sharp right and steeply downhill. At the bottom of the hill cross the Knighton-Llanfair Waterdine road and the railway and the bridge specially rebuilt over the Teme. Follow the riverside path and then up the steps into the Offa's Dyke Park by the stone commemorating the Opening. Through the Park to West Street by the Information Centre, left and your starting point is reached.

A pleasant short walk (A on map) may be had by cutting from point (2), (298728) to point (6), (285735) across the top of Kinsley Wood. It can be extended by walking on the Dyke from the latter point to the top of Panpunton Hill.

Just before the path would rejoin A488 Clun road it joins a loosely metalled surface with two horseshoe bends: the main route described above goes forward down at the first horseshoe and over the stile straight ahead. The Kinsley alternative goes forward up at the first horseshoe.

Climb with this and just beyond the first bend in 200 yards take a very steep track striking up on the left into the woods. Near the top of the slope, right at T junction with a broader track. Keep to this track as it crosses a summit, falls and starts to rise again gently. Avoid a prominent left turn but just beyond this take a left small green path at fork. Right on metalled track at T-junction and, at first bend, through gate straight ahead.

Half-left down field to cross stile by Offa's Dyke Path signpost and so back down the left side of the field towards Knighton.

Between Knighton and Lower Spoad west of Clun (Norman castle and ancient bridge) is some of the wildest and best of both Path and Dyke including the latter's highest point (1,408 feet). Springhill just north of this is the standard spot for visiting parties to see a 'good continuous stretch of Dyke'.

Area 7 West of Bishop's Castle and Kerry Hill Ridgeway

(A) 9, (B) 5½ and (C) 5 miles.

O.S. 1:50,000. 137; O.S. 1:25,000. SO 28.
Grid references are to these maps.

How to get there: These three walks start 4½ miles west of Bishop's Castle (22 miles from Shrewsbury on A488; Ludlow is 18 and Craven Arms 10 miles away). Detailed instructions to reach the starting point are given below. Valley Motors run a Shrewsbury-Bishop's Castle bus service but there is nothing nearer the route.

Refreshments: Town facilities at Bishop's Castle; Middle Knuck, on the Offa's Dyke Path ½ mile south of Churchtown, is now a Walker's Hostel providing dormitory accommodation and some meals by prior arrangement. Apart from this bring your own food and drink as there is nothing directly on the walks.

The high Dyke continues north of Clun until beyond the Kerry Hill ridgeway north of which it drops down to the plain of Montgomery and the Severn Valley. The Clun-Kerry Hill stretch is one of the most tiring to walk—the usual appellation of "switchback" explaining why. Sparsely populated, little visited, it remains one of the most exciting parts of the Path and the following walks are in a small way testing as well as most enjoyable. They start at a height of 1,300 feet and never drop below 900 and are over wild hilly remote country with wide views. Underfoot it is often wet and muddy.

Bishop's Castle, with its 1,000 years of history, is an attractive and busy little market town (a borough until 1967). Its hilly main street has the Parish church with Norman tower at one end and the 18th century Town Hall at the other and in between most of the architectural styles of the past 200 years.

To get to the starting point go down the main street of Bishop's Castle and turn right at the Parish Church. Continue on this narrow road for about 3 miles until Bishopsmoat is reached, noting on the right a well-preserved Norman motte. At the crossroads take the middle road labelled PANTGLAS, go past a telephone kiosk at Hazel Bank and park your car on the grass verge, (1) (258896), where the Offa's Dyke Path crosses the Kerry Hill Ridgeway.

AREA 7

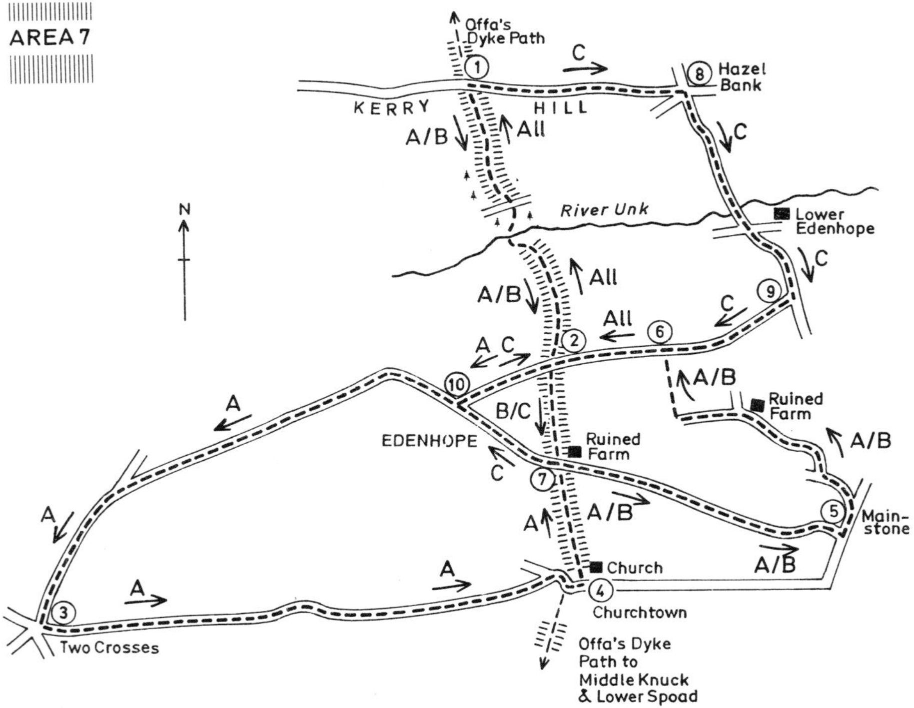
Offa's Dyke Path
KERRY HILL
Hazel Bank
River Unk
Lower Edenhope
N
EDENHOPE
Ruined Farm
Ruined Farm
Church
Churchtown
Main-stone
Two Crosses
Offa's Dyke Path to Middle Knuck & Lower Spoad
1
2
3
4
5
6
7
8
9
10
A/B
All
C
A
B/C

WALK A

Climb over the stile to the South, as the Offa's Dyke fingerpost bids you and clamber on to the path, which soon skirts a forest of conifers to your right, before entering it at a waymarked stile. The track now slopes quickly into Nut Wood, at the bottom of which lies the little River Unk, a tributary of the River Clun, which it joins at the town of that name, later to be swallowed up in the Teme. Cross the Unk by the plank bridge and make for the path on the Dyke, which can be seen climbing up the steep bank opposite. Once up the hill, the path soon levels out to reach the narrow road that runs at right angles to it along Edenhope Hill, (2) (263883). This is a good moment to stand and stare. As you draw breath, take in the spectacular scenery of the Clun Forest with Corndon Hill away to the North-East, and if you are birdwatchers, look out for buzzards soaring above Edenhope Hill.

Suitably refreshed turn right, leaving Offa's Dyke for a while, and enjoy the luxury of walking along the level grass-bordered road, which runs east-west. You are still over 1,300 feet above sea-level here and, although you will soon lose a little height as the road crosses a cattle-grid and becomes unfenced, you will still have the feeling of being on top of the world as, about 1¾ miles after leaving the Offa's Dyke Path, you come to Two Crosses, (3) (240868). At the crossroads take the left fork down a narrow road, which will soon drop into a well-wooded valley with splendid views of the tree-covered hillside opposite you to the south. This lonely, little-used road leads in 1½ miles down to Churchtown, (4) (264874), to use the rather grand name given by the O.S. to a hamlet of several houses, a white caravan and a church. Here the Offa's Dyke Path comes down from the north to the valley floor before quickly climbing again to the south (to reach Middle Knuck in ½ mile). The earliest settlers here were probably traders making a living out of supplying the needs of those who used the Dyke. The church is the parish church of Mainstone, a village a mile away to the east. Just before you reach the church, which is on your left-hand side, turn left on to the Offa's Dyke Path again, as it climbs sharply to the North. After about half a mile a wide grassy track crosses the path from the north-west. Turn right on to this track, once again taking your leave of Offa's Dyke. After walking to the south-east for a few hundred yards you will find that the track enters a field through an open gate. Keep close to the hedge, which will remain on your left-hand side and the track, which at times becomes a sunken lane under overarching trees, will take you to the village of Mainstone (5) (275876).

Mainstone is an isolated spot, named after a large boulder, which according to local tradition was used as a test of a man's strength. Turn left and walk on the metalled road for a hundred yards, then turn left again at the chapel. Follow the winding grassy track up to a barn on the skyline. The adjoining winding grassy track up to a barn on the skyline. The adjoining farm, now completely in ruins, once boasted the name of King Gwilliam. The track divides here. Take the path to the left and keep on it for about a quarter of a mile until it reaches a gate at the top of the hill. Climb over the gate and at once turn right on to a small path which skirts the hedge. Follow this field-path which, after passing a pond, leads to a gate on to the Edenhope Hill Road, (6) (267884). Turn left onto this road and you will soon see the Offa's Dyke stile on your right (2) which you will have crossed earlier. Back over the stile then, and retrace your steps down to the Unk valley. Pass over the plank and go back through Nut Wood. Before long you will see your car on the Kerry Hill Ridgeway (1) (258896).

WALK B

(This is a shortened version of Walk A, devised especially for those who, after reaching the country road that runs along Edenhope Hill (2) (263883), feel that they may have bitten off more than they can chew).

Cross the road and move South once again on the Path, which at this point runs along the Dyke and soon winds its way by easy stages over the top of Edenhope Hill. It is as well, along this stretch, to beware a number of rabbit holes in the Dyke. Before long you will come to a scene of desolation; on your left is a ruined farm, with the slate roof lying more or less intact on the ground, and on your right is a grove of gaunt, dead trees. Here the hill begins to fall away and you will soon find a grassy lane running transversely across your path, (7) (263878). Turn to the left here and leave Offa's Dyke; as you follow the grassy lane down to Mainstone. (For the details of the rest of this walk, look back at the directions given in Walk A).

WALK C

From the same starting point turn round and walk down the lane in an easterly direction, past the telephone kiosk to the crossroads, where you take the road to the right at Hazel Bank, (8) (269896). This road soon becomes a steep and narrow lane winding down to the Unk valley. Shortly after crossing the little river the road divides, the left-hand fork leading to the nearby Lower Edenhope Farm. Take the road half-right, which climbs sharply for about a quarter of a mile. At (9) (275887) the road takes a 90° turn to the right; if you were to go straight on, you would soon find yourself in a cul-de-sac, leading to a farm. Turn right then, and you will be on the Edenhope Hill Road, whose wide grassy borders offer the walker a pleasant alternative to the high hard road.

The gradient is easy, the views magnificent; Clun Forest opens up ahead, as the highest part of the road is reached. Soon a stile on the right indicates the place where the Offa's Dyke Path crosses the road, (2) (263883). Almost opposite, the Dyke rises to the South. Take to this path on the left, which here coincides with the Dyke and which almost immediately climbs up towards the nearby summit of Edenhope Hill. Beware the rabbit holes, which abound on this section of the path. Just before the path begins a sharp descent, you will pass a ruined farm on your left and the skeletons of dead trees on your right. A minute later, the path meets a wide grassy track, which crosses the path in a north-west south-easterly direction, (7) (263878). Leave the Dyke here, and turn right towards the north-west. Continue on this track for rather less than half a mile, where the track joins the Edenhope Hill Road at (10) (258882). Turn right again and walk along the hill road for about 300 yards until the Offa's Dyke stile comes into view on the left at (2) (263883).

The rest of the walk is on the long-distance path. Cross the stile and moving northwards drop down into the Unk valley. Before you lose much height, look up to the hilly country in the north-east, where, if you are lucky, you will be rewarded with a view of Corndon Hill on the skyline. The Dyke disappears for a while into the valley, but you will soon see the little river Unk, which you will cross by a plank. A way-marked stile points the way to a steep and slippery path through Nut Wood. Once up this well-wooded hill the path leaves the trees and rejoins the Dyke in open country. Together path and Dyke soon return the walker to the Kerry Hill Ridgeway.

The next stretches of Path going north are generally pleasant but unexciting. We pass east of and close to Montgomery (and later Welshpool), from both of which circular walks can easily be worked out. Then over Beacon Ring Hill Fort on Long Mountain to cross the Severn at Buttington and up the towpath of the old Montgomery Canal and the Severn itself, with the Breidden Hills prominent to your right. We regain high ground north of Llanymynech where old Roman mineral workings are to be found and continue north towards Oswestry (Area 8).

Area 8 Oswestry, Sweeney Mountain and Trefonen

(A) 12 miles, (B) and (C) about 9 miles each.

O.S. 1:50,000. 126; O.S. 1:25,000. SJ 22 (mostly) and SJ 23. Grid references are to these maps.

How to get there: By car: A483 Chester-Swansea trunk road; 2 miles off A5 London-Holyhead.

By rail to Gobowen on Chester-Shrewsbury line. Trains about every 2 hours, then frequent Crosville bus (2 miles).

Refreshments: Royal Oak at Treflach, two pubs and shop at Trefonen. Plenty of choice in Oswestry.

The Dyke has been intermittent for most of the stretch since Kerry Hill (Area 7) but is very evident again in the few miles to the old Oswestry racecourse which are included in this chapter.

Oswestry has a long history, ranging from a bloody battle between Penda of Mercia and Oswald of Northumbria in the 7th century to the expansion as Cambrian Railway headquarters in the 19th. At some unknown even earlier time was the construction of Wat's Dyke east of the town, whose course is interrupted by the conspicuous Iron Age earthwork of *Old Oswestry*. The railway has gone but the Norman *Castle* mound, the Dyke and earthwork remain. In the 18th century it was pointed out that the eclipses of the sun in Aries had been fatal to the town, for there were disastrous fires in 1542 and 1567, in both of which years the sun was eclipsed in that planet! But there have been many other fires since King John burnt the town in 1215.

To traverse any of Offa's Dyke from Oswestry one must follow a triangular route, and Trefonen is a good place at which to join the long-distance path. For a flying start, take the morning or early afternoon bus (Crosville D76, every weekday) from Oswestry to Trefonen; otherwise start the walk by the Welshpoool Road, turning into Penylan Lane at (1) (288292) just beyond the Brook Street signals.

Penylan Lane is narrow but not busy; for nearly half its length one can walk behind the hedge, along the edge of the playing fields,

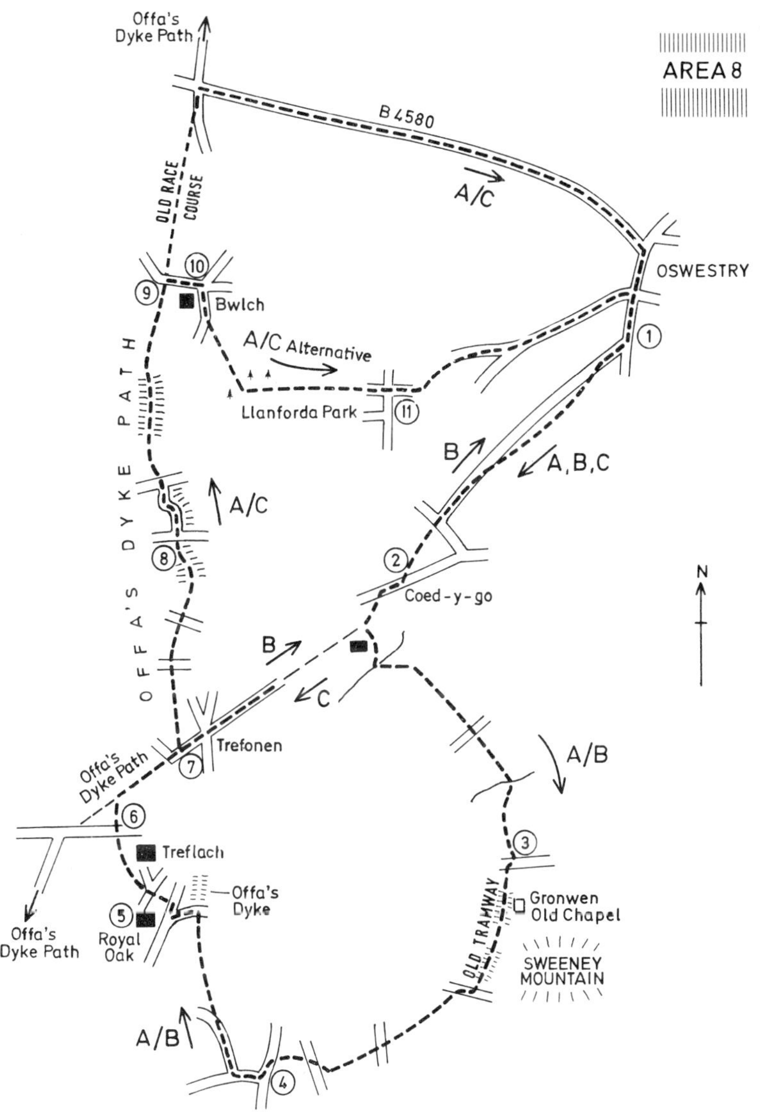
AREA 8
Offa's Dyke Path
B 4580
A/C
OLD RACE COURSE
OSWESTRY
10
9
Bwlch
A/C Alternative
1
OFFA'S DYKE PATH
Llanforda Park
11
B
A, B, C
A/C
8
2
Coed-y-go
N
B
C
Trefonen
7
A/B
Offa's Dyke Path
6
3
Treflach
Offa's Dyke
Gronwen Old Chapel
OLD TRAMWAY
5
Royal Oak
Offa's Dyke Path
SWEENEY MOUNTAIN
A/B
4

where rather surprisingly there is a public footpath. The lane ends at a T-junction: cross the stile ahead and at the end of the long field take the stile, not the gate, and so at the next stile reach the road at Coed-y-go (2) (273277). At the far end of a block of former cottages with large upstairs windows (built for weavers, perhaps?) a path from a tall stile crosses a field to a group of farm buildings (Gwern). To the right of these a stile marks the straight well-trodden path across the fields to Trefonen (2½ miles from the start by route C).

For walks (A) and (B) go through an iron fieldgate left of the Gwern buildings; the path skirts a boggy patch to a stile under a holly, then bears right to a concrete sleeper bridge before resuming its south-westerly direction, shown by stiles, to cross a road. In the second field beyond the road, strike across to the bottom right-hand corner; beyond the stile, turn right across the brook and climb the bank keeping a tall holly hedge on the left. At the far end of this hedge the path crosses a stile, then continues by the right-hand hedge in three fields to Gronwen (3) (278264).

From just beyond the double bend, follow a drive to a farm (the former chapel shown on the OS map has gone) and go through a gate between the Dutch barn and the other farm buildings. In the far corner of the field a stile leads to an embanked track—not a forgotten fragment of Wat's Dyke but a former tramway used to take coal from Trefonen to the limestone quarries around Nantmawr. It now makes a pleasant introduction to *Sweeney Mountain*, a modest height crowned by a folly (not accessible) and crossed by several paths.

When the embanked track reaches a road, turn right for a few yards to a fieldgate from which a path leads by a right-hand hedge. After crossing a brook, continue below the larch plantation to join a farm track running down to the field corner, where from a fieldgate and stile a green track runs forward past a stone house on the right. The track climbs through pleasant woodland (ignore a left downhill fork) until it reaches a gate and stone stile. The use of a thick stone slab placed vertically as the main part of a stile is common in these parts, but this one is unusual in having a hole through it to act as a step.

Bear right along the lane for some hundred yards, then left from a stile with steps by a visible path along one field to a road. Nearly opposite, a flight of steps shows the start of a continuing path, but as this is obstructed not only at the start but further on it is safer to follow the "Treflach" sign from the road junction below (4) (267249). Leave the road just beyond a quarry entrance, turning right by an access road (on which there may be parked lorries) leading to a well-trodden leftward path uphill past the remains of several small quarries. Continue in the same direction past several junctions until as the road curves left there is a large pasture field on the right. Cross this towards the house at the far corner, where a vertical-slab stile leads to a drive running sharply left: follow this round bends to the Trefonen road where the Royal Oak is opposite (5) (259255).

On heading northward from the Royal Oak notice the well-defined Dyke in the field opposite. The next path starts from a stile about 150 yards from the pub and crosses to a stile opposite the drive to Red House. Cross the rail on the left of the drive and in the pasture field, where the ridges of open field cultivation can be seen, keep just left of the knoll on which the farm stands, so as to reach a stile near the right-hand corner. In the next field keep left of the large open shed, cross a farm track and continue on the same line to a stile on the road (6) (253262), noting the wide view on the right where the Bickerton Hills of Cheshire can be seen across the plain.

From the opposite stile a path leads down to cross a brook by a stone slab. Beyond a stile in the corner and a small patch of wet woodland is another stone bridge: this is on the line of the Offa's Dyke Path leading to Trefonen, where there are two pubs and a shop. Just beyond the Post Office is the road along which the Path continues northward (7) (259267); beyond the central cross roads the direct way back to Oswestry (route B) starts along the "No Through Road" past the school. Route (C) has reached Trefonen by the same road in the opposite direction.

For the full walk, follow the Path waymarks: shortly the Dyke itself reappears near the bottom of the fields on the right. After crossing a road you bear right and follow the Dyke which becomes quite a massive bank on approaching Pentre-Shannel; but its line through Trefonen lends support to those who say that it was only an agreed boundary, for militarily it is in quite the wrong place for observing strangers approaching from Wales. Beyond the lane junction (8) (256279) the Dyke can be seen descending ahead (now facing towards Wales!) but the path alongside it has been lost and one has to follow the road through a smelly haulage yard to the site of Llanforda Mill, where the route crosses the River Morda.

On the climb through the wood the path is on a substantial causeway, a reminder that in the past the hill-dwellers returned from the mill with loads on their backs or on those of their animals. However, they would not have turned up the steep slopes as the Path does: look carefully for acorn signs here and if one seems to be missing from a junction go back to the last one, as there are numerous misleading tracks in the wood. After a short steep climb the path resumes its northward direction on a more gradual slope, with the Dyke itself in a commanding position close above it. On reaching a junction of five ways (9) (255298) go through the gate and turn sharp left and continue through Racecourse Wood to emerge on the Old Racecourse, a large area of common 1100 feet up on which to wander and enjoy the extensive views over Wales. The Dyke is now out of sight, down to the left.

The short way back to Oswestry is along B4580 but the bus service is only a market-day one; the walker who can contrive to have transport waiting here will avoid rather a dull walk. For an alternative which needs a little careful route-finding but is more varied and interesting, return to Racecourse Wood and bear left through the trees by one of the small tracks which converge at a step-stile overlooking a large house below; from here a path follows the top of the bank to the farm Bwlch (10) (257297). Continue ahead past the farm buildings and just beyond the pond go half-left through a field-gate to the furthest corner of a large field, then cross the right-hand ditch. A stile can now be seen to the left leading into a spinney; there is another stile on the far side of the spinney, not on the direct line of the path but somewhat to the right, and the way to it will be overgrown, but after emerging into the fields the rest of the route is easy.

Keep forward through two fieldgates: there is now a wide view extending from Cheshire round to the Long Mountain above Welshpool. When the ground starts to drop steeply, bear right to the gate at the bottom corner of the field. Beyond is the park of Llanforda Hall, a pleasant area with some fine trees; the Hall is no more, but the wall of the walled garden is conspicuous. The public path here is untraceable, but there is a clear way through a gate in a stone wall and then round the right-hand side of a wood, beyond which in the open park the way is roughly along the line of the power poles. After passing a wet wooded hollow, bear right so as to converge to a drive near the gate at its end (11) (274288). Cross the road and start along a drive but from the first lone tree bear left to a skyline stile, then make for the house at the far end of the long field. Minor roads lead in another mile to Oswestry.

The Path follows excellent stretches of Dyke north from Oswestry and past *Chirk Castle*—early 14th century but lived in continuously and now owned by the National Trust and open to visitors. After crossing Telford's A5 we reach the Llangollen Canal and turn along its towpath leaving the Dyke heading for the industrial area of Acrefair. Apart from a few traces near the north coast this is the last we see of the Dyke as the best of the rest of it is to be found amidst the industry of Wrexham and Rhos; the Path takes a more westerly course along the Clwydian Hills. The towpath soon crosses the magnificent Pontcysyllte Aqueduct over the Dee and most walkers will pass that way although the official route uses the Dee Bridge in the valley below—so the area covered in our next walks is reached.

Area 9 Llangollen, Valle Crucis, Eglwyseg and Dinas Bran

9 miles or 7 miles with optional extras.

O.S. 1:50,000. 117; O.S. 1:25,000. SJ 24.
Grid references are to these maps.

How to get there: By car: A542 to Valle Crucis (205442), car park serves both walks; A5 to Llangollen, car park between A5 and A539 reached from Market St. (214420) for longer route only.

By public transport: Rail to Ruabon and Crosville bus to Llangollen. Bryn Melyn Motors and Vale of Llangollen Tours, Llangollen operate local services.

Refreshments: Full range in Llangollen. Nothing elsewhere on route; Britannia Inn is 1 mile from Valle Crucis.

The Path passes north-east of Llangollen to climb to the *Panorama* or *Precipice Walk* (a small road in fact) and proceeds northwards. Our next walks link this stretch of the Path with the International Eisteddfod town of *Llangollen* and sites which tell the story of the Princes of Northern Powys, who held this frontier against Offa and then Norman invaders.

The route starts at the northern end of the bridge over the turbulent Dee, (1) on map (215422), the only notable ancient feature in Llangollen. Fifty yards east of the bridge a road to Minera, World's End and Eglwyseg turns sharply uphill and swings left below the Llangollen feeder of Telford's Shropshire Union Canal. Leave the road before crossing the hump-back bridge and follow the towpath north-westwards to where the A542 crosses it. Continuing along the towpath to the next bridge over the canal, (1 mile in all on the towpath), and turning back up the A542 for a hundred yards provides a pleasant way to the gate on the bend which is marked as the access to the local Rifle Range, (2) (208435). A field track from this gate leads to a path which continues to the bank of the Eglwyseg brook opposite *Valle Crucis Abbey,* and turns down to cross a footbridge just beyond the ruins. The path continues along the side of a field of caravans, providing rather incongruous neighbours for the finest monastic ruin in North Wales, then turns

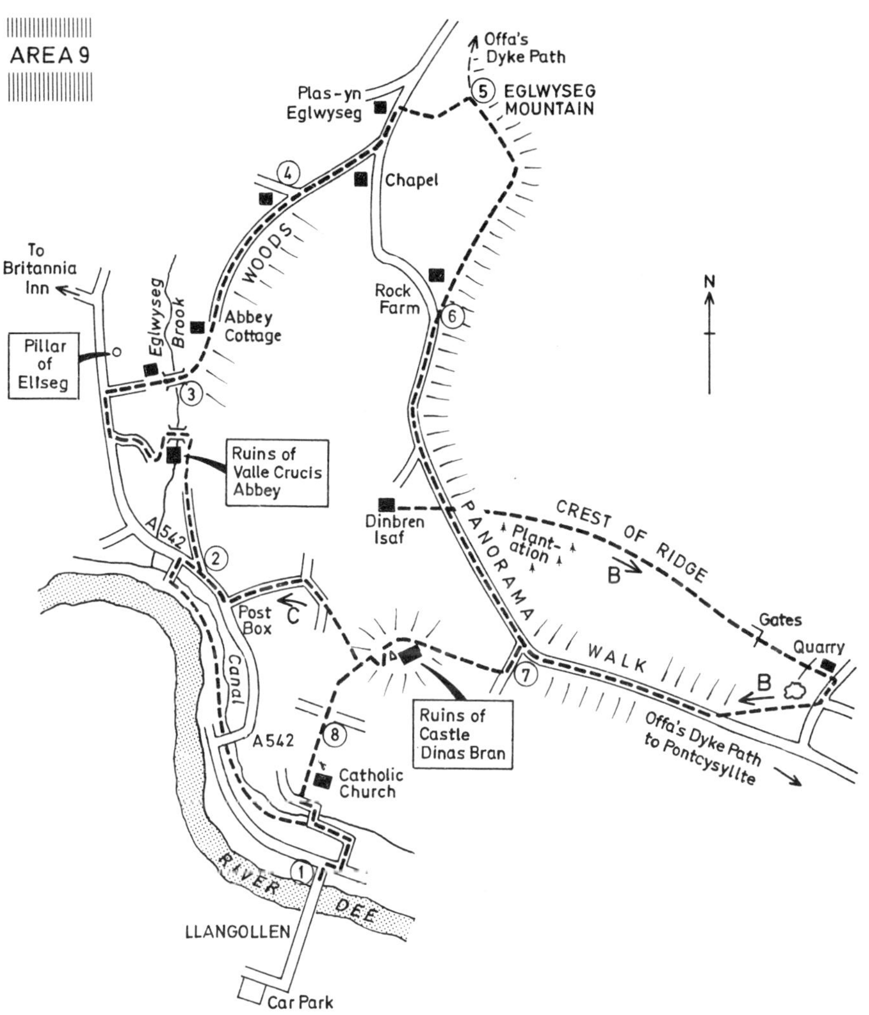

AREA 9
Offa's Dyke Path
Plas-yn Eglwyseg
5
EGLWYSEG MOUNTAIN
4
Chapel
WOODS
To Britannia Inn
Eglwyseg Brook
Rock Farm
6
N
Abbey Cottage
Pillar of Eliseg
3
Ruins of Valle Crucis Abbey
Dinbren Isaf
PANORAMA
CREST OF RIDGE
Plantation
A542
2
B
Post Box
C
Gates
Quarry
Canal
WALK
7
B
Ruins of Castle Dinas Bran
8
A542
Offa's Dyke Path to Pontcysyllte
Catholic Church
1
RIVER DEE
LLANGOLLEN
Car Park

left to the carpark and entrance.

The Abbey is maintained as an Ancient Monument, open throughout the year. Among the architectural details in the Abbey it is worth noting the finely carved tombstone of Madog ap Griffith. He was the grandson of the Madog who founded this Cistercian Abbey in 1201, and was himself the last Welsh prince who was able to rule Northern Powys effectively from Dinas Bran. Much of the castle masonry there seems to date from his period.

Continuing up the track which provides access to the carpark and turning right on the main road, the *Pillar of Eliseg* can be seen on a green mound on the right-hand side, two fields along. It is the remains of a 9th century memorial cross from which the valley, and the Abbey, took their names of 'the Vale of the Cross'. The faint inscription honoured Eliseg, Offa's contemporary and traced the ancestry of the ancient kings of Powys back to Vortigern and to his wife's father, Magnus Maximus, the commander of the legions in Britain, who was killed in 383 A.D. trying to make himself Emperor of Rome.

From the pillar you retrace your steps a hundred yards to the little lane down to a farm building, and down across the field to another footbridge over the Eglwyseg brook, (3) (205444). From this the path climbs to the left, crosses a ladder stile and follows the hedge northwards. The route turns right along the drive which runs from Abbey Cottage to the track running through the woods on the lower slopes of Fron Fawr and turns left to continue northwards along it.

This pleasant track continues for almost a mile, passing a farm and a few scattered houses before it joins the very minor metalled road from the A452, (4) (208458), and continues eastwards along it for another half a mile to the Eglwyseg chapel-of-ease at its junction with the road from Llangollen to World's End.

It is possible to save almost a mile of harder walking by turning right up this road to where the Offa's Dyke Path joins it above Rock Farm, (6) (218453), but to get a better impression of this stretch of the long-distance route, where it runs along the scree below the dramatic white crags of the scarp of Eglwyseg Mountain, turn left down the road to the farm buildings in the bottom of the valley.

There is a remarkable difference between the landscapes produced by the older Silurian rocks around Llangollen and these Carboniferous limestone crags to the north and east of them. The Silurian mudstones, flags and shales form steep but rounded hills, with few outcrops of bare rock, providing rough grazings for cattle and sheep, among spreads of gorse and bracken, where the sheer limestone crags are capped by sandstones and grits forming bleak, open, heather and bilberry-covered grouse moors.

Opposite the last farm building at Plas-yn-Eglwyseg, a right-of-way through a farm gate leads up into a hollow, crosses it into a field on the left to follow the hedge below the wood and join the Offa's Dyke Path at the ruins of Pen-yr-erw, (5) (220463). The limestone scree, below the sheer scarp, is embedded in red clay and carries more varieties of plants, with yew and mountain ash trees, dog violets, rock-rose and yellow wort among the flowers. Jackdaws and kestrels nest in crevices in the cliffs above.

From Pen-yr-erw we turn right. In the other direction the Offa's Dyke Path climbs steadily northwards along Llwybr-y-Fuwych, the old drovers' track to the market of Wrexham. Turning south into the hollow and slanting up into the scree covered slope beyond, our route reaches the thousand-foot contour, four hundred feet above the Eglwyseg brook, before it descends to other derelict buildings in the next hollow and continues along a broad track to join the Eglwyseg road above Rock (or Tan-y-graig) Farm, (6).

The route follows this road for half a mile before the road turns down to Llangollen at a point where another metalled track continues on through a gate. This is the start of the 'Panorama Walk' laid out in Llangollen's expansive 19th century era as a resort, when George Borrow made it his headquarters for his exploration of 'Wild Wales'. Our route follows another mile and a half of the Panorama Walk before turning off to climb the isolated hill of Dinas Bran, which appears to the right after we top the second gentle rise.

A detour over the tops. (B) The steady trickle of cars in summer may add to the restlessness of those walkers who would prefer to be up on the top of the limestone scarp. In ½ mile from the Dinas Bran turn, just before the ground begins to fall away more steeply on the right, a path through Dinbren Isaf farm comes out at a gate on that side (221441) and opposite a waymarked track slants up to the left and climbs one of the deep gullies in the face of the scarp. The path then follows an old wall and continues up to a stile in a fence. Turn right along broad track along the top side of the Eglwyseg plantation. This track swings left and soon forks up left to reach a gate in a wire fence. Turn right to reach a crest of the ridge (at 236438) above the 1,300 foot contour. From here the track commands views out over the towns and villages of the North Wales coalfield to the Cheshire plain, as it leads down to a field corner with two gates. Follow the track through the rightmost: where the path becomes boggy continue with it with wall on left (keeping well to right of white houses) to reach drive to a small road. Turn right: in ¼ mile just beyond the junction with the lane coming up from Acrefair, another path along the slope to the right provides a short-cut (keep left of an old quarry and avoid turns to right) to the Panorama Walk at the point where the Offa's Dyke Path, coming up from the south, joins it. From here it is a mile and a half back along the Panorama Walk to the Dinas Bran approach, and the whole circuit adds more than three miles and a stiff five hundred foot climb to the walk).

The route to *Dinas Bran* leaves the Panorama Walk along another metalled lane coming steeply up from Llangollen on the neck of the spur, (7) (227433), but leaves it after a short distance over a stile to the right, from which it aims across the hollow for the path which can be seen ascending the steep slope of the spur towards the ruins. When this ascent eases it is best to keep to the right, along the crest of the steep slope for the easiest crossing of the deep defensive ditch which also seems to have been the quarry for most of the stone from which the castle was built. This way leads through the narrow gatehouse entrance to the level grassy platform of the courtyard, around which stand the battered remains of the great hall, towers and curtainwalls of the 13th century castle. The site had been occupied by the fortifications of earlier princes of Powys, and the name of Dinas Bran and the fainter earthworks surrounding it suggest that it may have been occupied in the Dark Ages, and perhaps in even earlier periods when security was more important than comfort or ease of access.

From Dinas Bran the line of Offa's Dyke Path can be traced beyond where it descends at Trevor to link up briefly with the Llangollen Canal, on its approach to where Telford's great cast-iron aqueduct, on its pillars 120 feet high, can be seen striding across the Dee valley. Beyond that the Path comes to Offa's Dyke itself, pushed back here onto the edge of the plain, out of sight of the princes of Powys.

The path from the other end of the castle, overlooking Llangollen, descends even more steeply on a zig-zag course, then continues across a slight hollow to swing left along the hedge at the end of the open ground, through a gate into a lane, and down across another lane, (8) (217428). Where the lane bends sharply left, continue down through the wicket gate ahead, along the hedge to another gate into a path which runs between the school playing fields and the Catholic Chapel. This leads back to the Eglwyseg road at the canal bridge, completing the circuit, and back to the bridge over the Dee and

Llangollen's main streets.

A Shorter 7 mile Circuit (C) can be walked by starting from the car park at Valle Crucis, walking the route from there to Dinas Bran, but returning without descending to Llangollen:

At the foot of the steep descent from Dinas Bran, (at 218 430), look out for a path turning down through the bracken on the right, to a swing-gate into a field. The path runs down alongside the hedge, and along the bottom side of the field to a stile by a field gate onto the Eglwyseg road. Five hundred yards up this, fork left along the lane which leads down to the main road at the Ty-du post-box (209 435). Just along the main road to the right is the gate and the track to the Rifle Range, and to the path back to Valle Crucis by way of the footbridge across the Eglwyseg brook, (3) (205 444).

The Panorama Walk leads to World's End and then the Path crosses desolate (and fairly trackless) moorland to the village of Llandegla. 3 miles more and you are at the foot of the Clwyds.

(A) 5 miles and (B) 7 miles, with extensions of (C) 2½ and (D) 2 miles.

O.S. 1:50,000. 116; O.S. 1:25,000. SJ 16 for main routes, extensions go on to SJ 06, 07, 17.
Grid references are to these maps.

How to get there: By car: Leave Mold on A541 Denbigh road; in 5½ miles go left for Nannerch and immediately left, Llandyrnog turn; in 2½ miles park at the highest point, (1) (139669). For extensions cars may be left at Bodfari or Afonwen on A541.

By public transport: Crosville Mold-Denbigh service serves Afonwen and Bodfari; the Denbigh-Llangwyfan Hospital route (some buses go on to Ruthin) terminates one mile from the suggested car park but only ½ mile from the nearest point on the route, (3) (131664). No Sunday buses.

Refreshments: Inns and village shops at Bodfari, Afonwen and Llandyrnog (2½ miles west of car park).

The 14 miles between the foot of the Clwyds and Bodfari are as exhilarating as any on the whole route with ridge walks, peaks, hill-forts and views as far as Snowdonia. Mold, Ruthin and Denbigh are within reach and it is in the northern part of this setting that the tenth group of walks are located.

From the car park referred to, (1) (139669), take wicket gate on right into Llangwyfan/Clwyd Forest. Offa's Dyke Path is the highest on the right (not a forest ride) and follows the edge of the woods below the fence along the crest of the ridge. Cross stile and up grassy track to the ramparts of the southern corner of the hillfort of *Penycloddiau*, ⅔mile from the start of the walk.

The circuit of the ramparts is a full mile, in places they are tripled and the interior covers 50 acres. The views in all directions are extensive. Offa's Dyke Path goes across the centre of the enclosure. The full circuit of the ramparts is **not** included in the route mileage!

Cross the north end of the ramparts and follow grass paths through heather slowly dropping in under a mile to a pass at over 1,000 feet, (2) (121690). Ahead is the northernmost of the Clywdian range, Moel-y-Parc with its television mast. Here four ancient roadways cross, Offa's Dyke Path descending to Bodfari being the one going

AREA 10
To Caerwys
A 541
Afonwen
To Mold
Candy Mill
Offa's Dyke Path to Prestatyn
Track of old railway
Church
Bodfari
A 451
R. Wheeler
The Grove
OFFA'S DYKE PATH
TV Mast
Moel-y-Parc
C
D
A/B
Peny-Cloddiau
To Nannerch
Car Park
A
B
Tan-y Graig
Moel Arthur
Offa's Dyke
N
1
2
3
4
5
6
7

left at 90° (this route is described later). This walk, however, takes the route **very** sharp left. This contours, very slightly dropping for two miles. About ¼ mile before the end of this stretch, the track forks and the left (lower) fork should be taken; this soon swings left and reaches the Nannerch-Llandrynog road again, (3) (131664) just above Tan-y-Graig (the nearest point to the Llangwyfan Hospital bus route).

Two routes are possible from here; the shorter (A) to complete the 5 mile round, is to re-enter the forest immediately on the left and take the Forestry road directly uphill with stream below on your right. Soon, for part of the way, there is a lower, grassier alternative on the right which winds with the Forestry road and eventually rejoins it. In 2/3 mile this reaches the car park by the road, (1).

For the longer route (B) cross stream by road. After 100 yards, through gate on right and head diagonally left uphill to edge of field. Follow edge, through gate on left and left uphill to two pine trees, leaving farm on right. Cross farm drive and take green lane opposite uphill. When this reaches col, contour to left, aiming at prominent hawthorn on track through bracken. Eventually join broad track, coming from right, in patch of trees. Forward through gate and contour on track right round head of valley, on right, to reach tarred road. Then left and upwards to top of the pass between Moel Llys-y-Coed and Moel Arthur, (4), (146657).

The route now rejoins the Offa's Dyke Path to go northwards along the crest of the Clwyds. First the steep climb to the top of the tiny but well-defined hill-fort on Moel Arthur. From car park, follow white posts (placed to allow recovery of eroded slopes) up and over shoulder of hill fort, to right of the summit. From here you can cross to the summit which with its triple lines of defences and steep gradients on all but the northern side is indeed impressive. Clwyd County Council have bought the hill and designated it as a country park. Return to white posts and follow them down to reach the car park at (1) in over ½ mile.

The two extensions are the Offa's Dyke Path from Bodfari to the pass at point (2) of 2½ miles (C), and the route from that point northwards to the A541 at Afonwen—2 miles (D). If travelling by bus, outward from Bodfari to (2) and return to Afonwen is recommended, inserting of course the round described above starting and finishing at point (2). If a car is used the National Footpath to and from Bodfari, leaving the vehicle at this point, is pleasant. We have as yet not found a satisfactory route from Afonwen to Bodfari (see, however, under Afonwen extension below) and would be pleased to hear of one to complete this northern circuit.

Route C

From the Downing Arms at Bodfari, (5) (098702), turn right on main road for 50 yards, left through gate immediately followed by stile. Cross old railway track and river Wheeler to small road. Left up lane for 200 yards, then right and immediately left to road rising towards TV mast on skyline. Take first right turn at pillar box (The Grove) and immediately past house on left cross stile (with acorn mark and concrete Offa's Dyke marker).

Cross field to next stile with Grove Farm on right, cross stile and contour forward with wire fence on left, cross next stile and climb to the left to old stile. Continue climbing diagonally to acorn-marked stile, cross this and climb further diagonally right to stile by gate at head of sunken green lane. After 200 yards join larger track and continue climbing, then contouring along hillside on unfenced track which eventually drops to cross stream just below farm (Tynewydd), (6) (114692), and rises again to iron gate. This part of the track is roughly metalled.

Beyond this the track has hedge on left, then on both sides and soon reaches a stile above ruined farm buildings. From here it is an easy climb to the pass to join the circular walk, (2) (121690).

The Afonwen route (D) is left from this point (straight forward from the Offa's Dyke Path coming northwards to the pass) along broad unmetalled track leading towards the TV mast. In ½ mile it acquires a metal surface and descends steeply to reach the A541, (7) (131716).

From here the little 'planned town' at *Caerwys,* an Edward I creation with a late Decorated church, may be reached in a mile. Turn left on the A541 and in ¼ mile take the footpath right by Pwllgwyn Hotel to Caerwys. It is possible to go by small roads westwards from here for 3 miles to join the Offa's Dyke Path on the north side of Cefn Du (094732) and then southwards for 2½ miles to Bodfari. The quickest route from Afonwen to Bodfari is 1½ miles west on A541 then take minor road left at Candy Mill; in 2 miles the Long Distance path is reached just east of Bodfari.

Going north from Bodfari the Path crosses lower hills until it emerges on a cliff edge two miles south-west of Prestatyn with sands and contemporary holiday appurtenances between you and the sea. On to the southern end of Prestatyn; down Fford-Las—the main street—past station, shops and candy floss stalls to the sea front. You have arrived at the end of Offa's Dyke Path!

Bibliography

The following books provide further information about the Long Distance Foothpath:

'Through Welsh Border Country' by Mark Richards (Thornhill Press).

'The O.D.A. Book of Offa's Dyke Path' by Frank Noble (Offa's Dyke Services—revised reprint 1981).

'Offa's Dyke Path' by John B. Jones (HMSO).

'A Guide to Offa's Dyke Path' by Christopher J. Wright (Constable).

'The Offa's Dyke Path' by Arthur Roberts (Ramblers' Association booklet).

The historical feature can be studied in great depth in Sir Cyril Fox's 'Offa's Dyke' (Oxford University Press for British Academy) and 'Offa's Dyke Reviewed' by Frank Noble, ed. M. Gelling (BAR British Series 114, 1983).

For background on the Welsh Marches, Maxwell Fraser's 'Welsh Border Country' (Batsford) is invaluable.

'Rural Landscapes of the Welsh Borderland' by Dorothy M. Sylvester (Macmillan)

Regional Guides to Ancient Monuments—3. Midlands, 4. South Wales, 5. North Wales; also separate guides to the main monuments under the guardianship of the Dept. of the Environment (HMSO).

The Offa's Dyke Association publishes and sells other guide material, strip maps, accommodation lists, postcards, badges, T-shirts etc.

Details of these and of membership are available (s.a.e. please) from O.D.A., West Street, Knighton, Powys, LD7 1EW.

Some Useful Addresses

Countryside Commission, John Dower House, Crescent Place, Cheltenham, Glos., and its Office for Wales, 8 Broad Street, Newtown, Powys.

English Tourist Board, 4 Grosvenor Gardens, London S.W.1.

Wales Tourist Board, Welcome House, Llandaff, Cardiff.

Ramblers' Association, 1/5 Wandsworth Rd., London SW8 2LJ.

Youth Hostels Association (England and Wales), Trevelyan House, 8 St. Stephen's Hill, St. Albans, Herts.

Ancient Monuments Branch, Inspectorate, Welsh Office, Cathays Park, Cardiff.

Clwyd-Powys Archaeological Trust Ltd., 7a Church Street, Welshpool, Powys.

The Commons, Open Spaces and Footpaths Preservation Society, 25a Bell Street, Henley-on-Thames, Oxfordshire.